Robert Pęczkowski

Colour profiles
Artur Juszczak

Lockheed P-38 LIGHTNING Early Versions

Dla Agi i Tomka

Published in Poland
in 2017
by STRATUS sp.j.
PO Box 123,
27-600 Sandomierz 1
Email:
office@wydawnictwostratus.pl

www.wydawnictwostratus.pl

as
MMPBooks,
Email:
office@mmpbooks.biz

2017 MMPBooks
www.mmpbooks.biz

ISBN:
978-83-65281-31-9

Editor in chief
Roger Wallsgrove
Editorial Team
Bartłomiej Belcarz
Artur Juszczak
Robert Pęczkowski

Colour profiles
Artur Juszczak

Scale plans
Dariusz Karnas

DTP
Stratus sp. j.

Printed by
Drukarnia Diecezjalna,
ul. Żeromskiego 4,
27-600 Sandomierz
www.wds.pl
marketing@wds.pl
PRINTED IN POLAND

Table of contents

Acknowledgement

Author wish to acknowledge the kind help of the following: Steven Dickey, Tomasz J. Kopański, the late Arthur Lochte, Robert Panek.

Introduction

Lockheed designed the P-38 in response to a February 1937 specification from the United States Army Air Corps (USAAC).

The Lockheed design staff was headed by Hall L. Hibbard. The second designer was the soon-to-be famous Clarence L. "Kelly" Johnson. They were considering many different designs, but Hibbard and Johnson finally decided on a twin-boom design with each boom extending aft of the engine, the pilot sitting in an enclosed cockpit in a central nacelle. The new 1150 hp Allison V-1710C twelve-cylinder liquid-cooled engine with an exhaust-driven turbosupercharger was used, one mounted in each boom. The central nacelle contained a forward-firing armament of one cannon and four 0.50-in machine guns. One big advantage of the twin-boom layout was the possibility of installing the armament in the central nacelle, which allowing sighting of the parallel streams of fire up to the maximum range of 1000 yards, without synchronizing gear. Tail surfaces consisted of a fin and rudder at the end of each boom and a horizontal tail plane and elevator between the booms. It was anticipated that the twin fin and rudder tail assembly would increase the effective aspect ratio of the tail plane by the endplate effect. Fowler flaps were also fitted.

P-38 concept design original drawings as were shown in patent application.

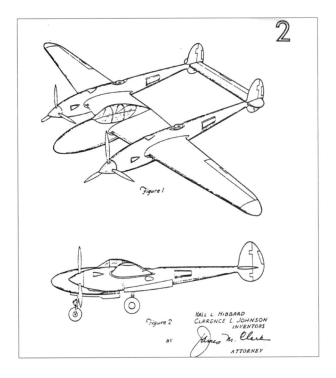

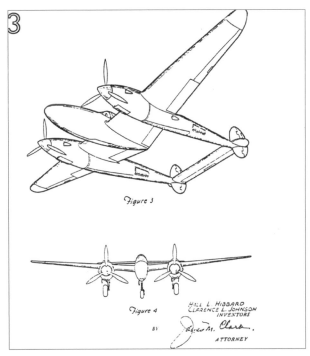

Lockheed XP-38

The project was given the company designation Model 22-64-01. Designers promised a maximum speed of over 400 mph. Although the USAAC was somewhat sceptical about so radical a design, when the Model 22 won Design Competition X-608 on 23 June 1937, Lockheed received a contract for one XP-38 prototype (No 37-457) for US$ 163,000, though Lockheed's own costs on the prototype would add up to US$ 761,000. Construction began in July 1938. No armament was installed on the aircraft.

The XP-38 aircraft was completed in December of 1938. Lt. Kelsey finally took the XP-38 into the air for the first time on 27 January 1939. Maximum speed was 413 mph at 20,000 feet, and an altitude of 20,000 feet could be reached in 6.5 minutes. Service ceiling was 38,000 feet. The aircraft was equipped with Allison V-1710-11 and -15 engines (C-series).[1]

The XP-38 crashed on 11 February 1929 during an attempted record transcontinental flight and was scrapped.

---

1   C-series engines had the crankshaft at the centre and the gear housing was a tapered cylinder with epicyclic gear inside. F-series engines used on the later models had the higher propeller shaft.

Two photos of the XP-38 sole prototype at Burbank, California, 1939. (Lockheed)

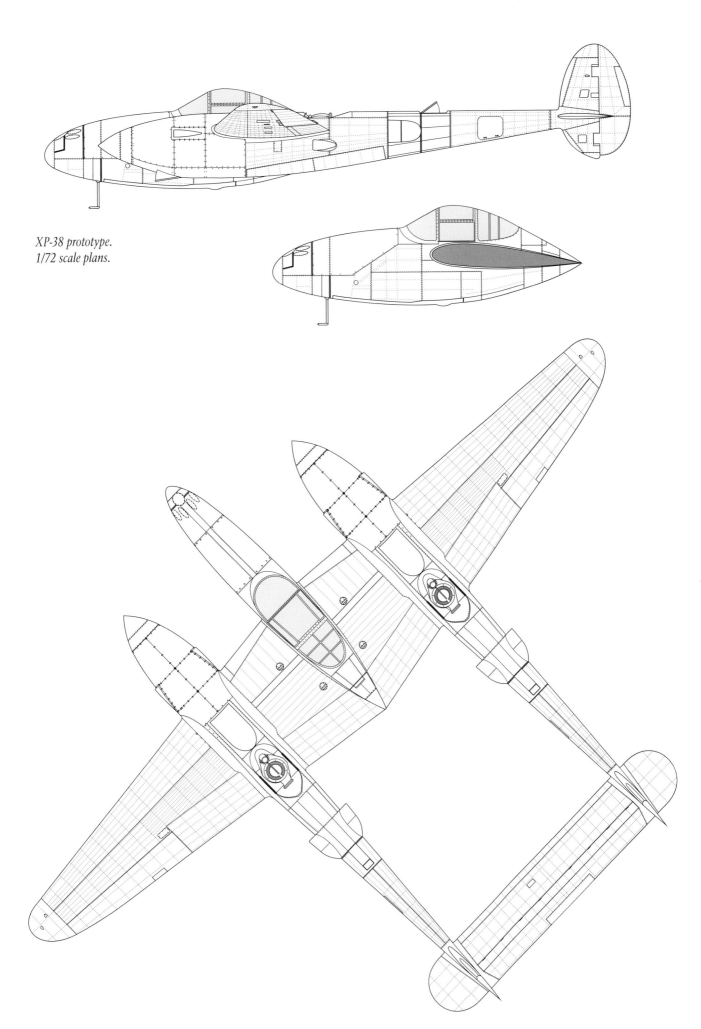

XP-38 prototype.
1/72 scale plans.

XP-38 prototype.
1/72 scale.

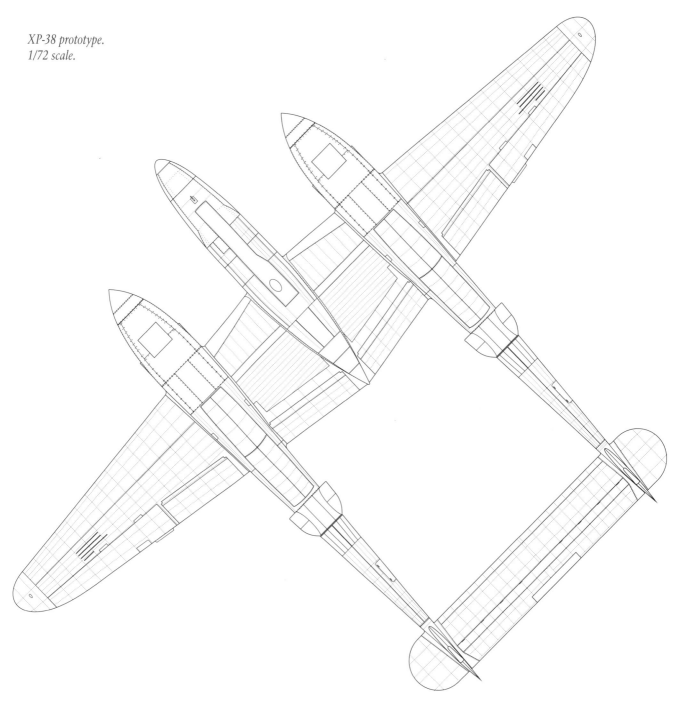

XP-38 at Lockheed plant in Bur-
bank California.
(Lockheed)

Lockheed YP-38

O n 27 April 27 1939 a Limited Procurement Order for 13 YP-38 service test aircraft was issued. Price was agreed at US$ 134,284 each. The Lockheed designation was Model 122-62-02.

The YP-38 was redesigned for production by receiving a pair of 1150 hp Allison V-1710-27 and -29 (F-series, F2R and F2L)[2] engines equipped with B-2 turbosuperchargers. The chin-mounted lip intake under the propeller spinner was replaced by a pair of cooling intakes. Also, enlarged coolant radiators were introduced on both sides of the tail booms.

Armament was revised to substitute two 0.30-in machine guns for two of the four 0.50-in machine guns, and a 37-mm Browning M9 cannon with 15 rounds was substituted for the 20-mm weapon.

During tests, most YP-38s were flown without guns installed. Also, the YP-38 was lighter (14,348 lbs.) than the overweight XP-38 thanks to structural changes.

The first YP-38 flew on 16 September 1940. In March 1940, the Army received its first YP-38 for service trials. Production lagged behind schedule, and all thirteen YP-38s had not been completed until June of 1941.

During trials, the YP-38s ran into a problem in which the tail began to buffet during high speed dives, and the nose would tuck under, steepening the dive. This problem was solved by adding large wing-root fillets at the points where the wings joined the fuselage.

The first of thirteen YP-38s. Note the cuffs on the propeller blades, but were removed soon. (USAFM)

---

2   To combat torque, the propellers rotated in opposite directions, a special version of the Allison engine being produced with a left-hand rotating propeller shaft.

YP-38 prototype.
1/72 scale plans.

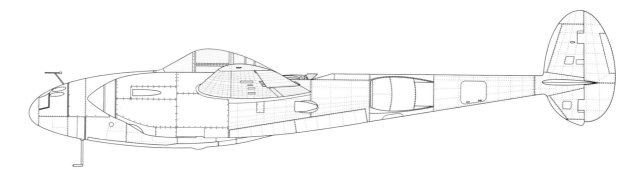

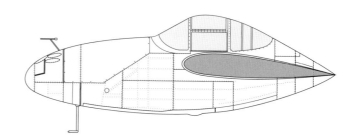

Two photos of the YP-38.
Note different engine na-
celles, than the XP-38.
(Lockheed)

Lightnings for RAF

Lightning I

In France in spring of 1939, the *Comité du Matériel* and the *Etat Major* had been looking at the P-38 as a possible substitute for the Breguet 700, Potez 671, and Sud-Est S.E.100 twin-engined fighters. Then in April 1940, the Anglo-French Purchasing Committee[3] ordered 667 P-38 fighters. The two versions were the Model 322-61-03 (or 322-F) for France and 322-61-04 (or 322-B) for Britain.

Both the British and French delegations insisted that the Lockheed P-38 be equipped with Allison engines without turbosuperchargers and with strictly right-handed rotation. This was because they wanted the engines to be interchangeable with those of the Curtiss H. 81A Tomahawk which had been ordered by both Britain and France in great numbers. The delegation was also aware of the problems currently being experienced by the War Department in the delivery of turbosuperchargers, and did not want to run the risk of delays since they wanted all the planes delivered in less than a year. It turned out that this decision was mistaken. There is also a suggestion that the US did not want to sell turbocharged engines to non-US buyers.

Both Model 322s were powered by Allison V-1710-C15 engines without turbosuperchargers that were rated at 1010 hp at 14,000 feet. These aircraft were to have both engines rotating in the right-handed sense. Also the French version was to have French (i.e. metric-calibrated) instruments, French-built radios and French-supplied armament, and were to have throttles which operated in the "French fashion"[4].

---

3   The Anglo-French Purchasing Committee was an Associated bodies of The Anglo-French Supreme War Council, which was established to oversee joint military strategy at the start of the Second World War.

4   In the reverse direction from British/American throttles.

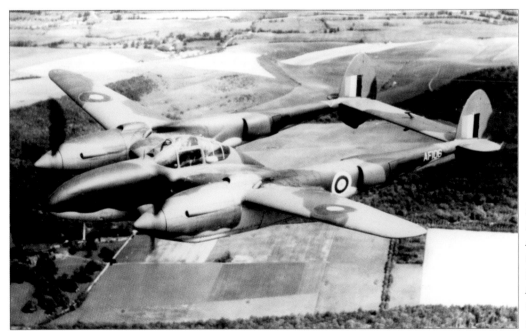

Perfect view of the Lightning I serial AF106. Note the shape of the cowling with C-series engine. Also the lack of the turbo-supercharger is evident.

After the fall of France in June of 1940, the entire contract for the Model 322s was taken over by Britain. By July of 1941, the RAF recognized that there probably would be a need for high altitude capabilities, and the original contract was amended to provide for the delivery of 143 Lightning Is[5] with the originally-specified V-1710-15 un-turbosupercharged engines, with the remaining 524 aircraft[6] to be delivered as Lightning IIs (Model 322-60-04) with turbosupercharged V-1710-F5L and -F5R engines.

The first three Lightnings arrived in the UK by sea transport in March of 1942. P-38 serial AF105 was sent to Cunliffe-Owen Aircraft Limited at Swaythling, Southampton for examination and experiments. P-38 serial AF106 was sent to the A&AEE at Boscombe Down for flight evaluation. Lightning I serial AF107 went to the Royal Aircraft Establishment at Farnborough for experiments and evaluation. The performance of the aircraft was very poor, and the RAF refused any further deliveries of the Lightning I.

The remaining 140 Lightning Is of the British contract were completed by Lockheed and were taken over by the USA and designated P-322-I. Aircraft were sent to a special modification centre in Dallas, Texas where they were adapted for US service, most of them being used as trainers and for various experimental roles. They retained their original British serial numbers. Twenty of the P-322s retained their V-1710-C15 engines (USAAF designation V-1710-33) with unhanded propellers. The rest of the P-322s were fitted with handed engines (V-1710-27 and -29) but were not given turbosuperchargers. They were used as a trainers with reduced armament (no cannon).

Lightning I side view.   5   British military serials AE978 to AE999 and AF100 to AF220.
1/72 scale.   6   Serials AF221 to AF744.

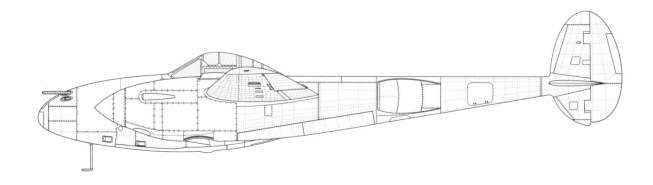

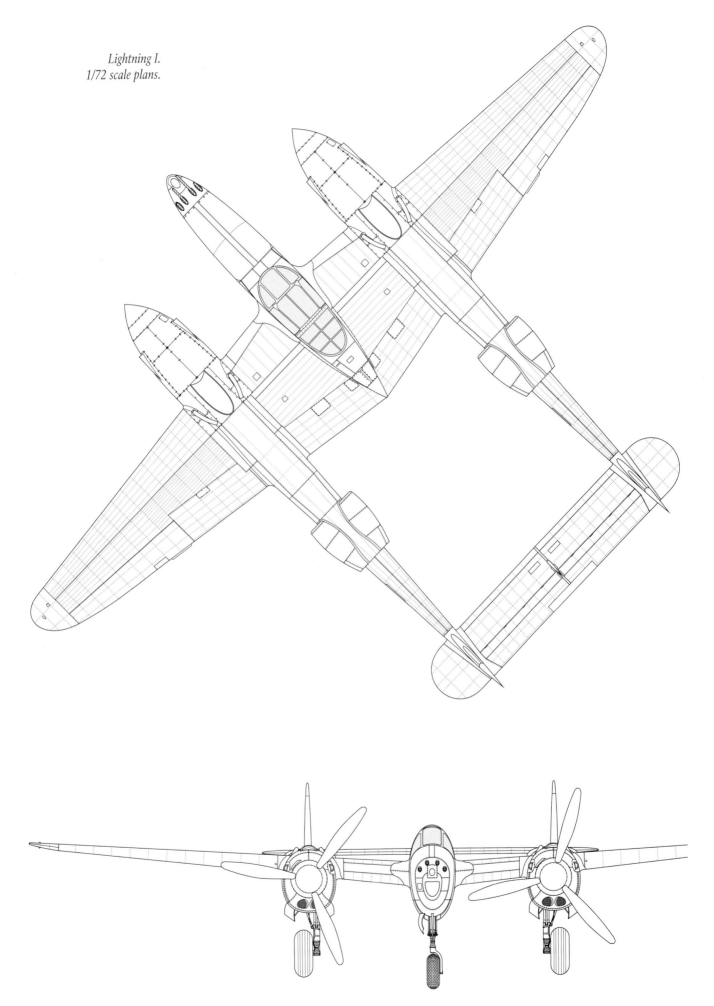

Lightning I.
1/72 scale plans.

11

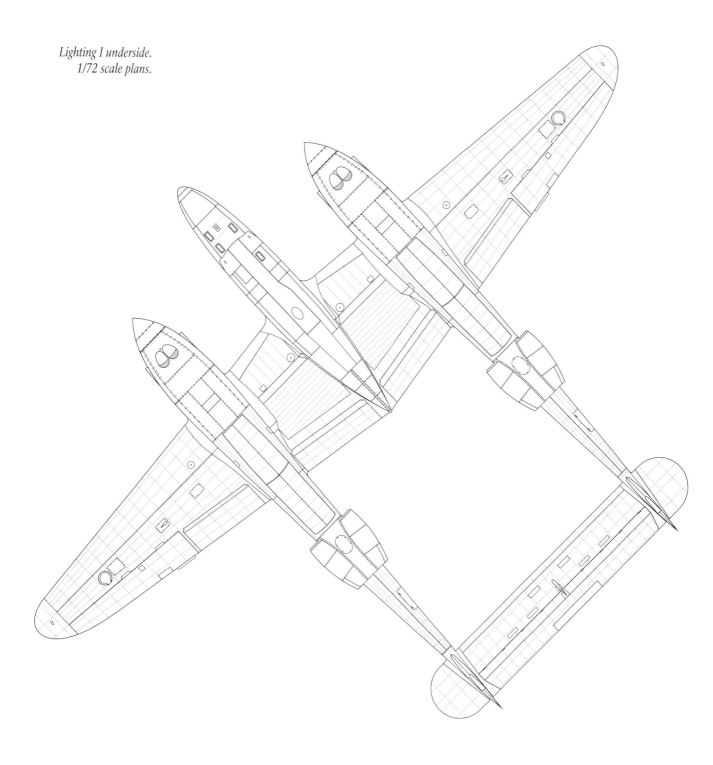

Lightning II

Only one Lightning II (AF221) was completed. It was taken over by the USAAF as P-38F-13-10, painted with US national markings, but retaining its British serial number. It was used by Lockheed for the testing of smoke- laying canisters on racks between the booms and the nacelle, and for the air-dropping of two torpedoes from the same racks.

Twenty-eight other British-ordered aircraft were completed as P-38F-13-LO for the USAAF, 121 as P-38F-15-LO, 174 as P-38G-13-LO, and 200 as P-38G-15-LO. The Army placed an order for 66 P-38 fighters on 20 September, 1939.

Lightning I serial AF979 was never sent to UK.

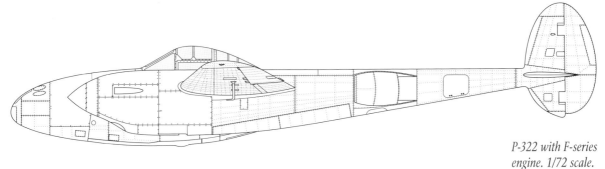

P-322 with F-series engine. 1/72 scale.

Lockheed P-38 (P-38-LO)

P-38-LO landing in one of the US bases. (USAFM)

Twenty-nine aircraft were delivered as P-38-LO[7] (company Model 222-62-02), the rest from the order were finished as XP-38A (one) and P-38D (36).

The P-38 had the same engines as the XP-38, but armament was changed to one 37-mm cannon and four 0.50-in machine guns. Armour plate and bulletproof glass was added for pilot protection. Fluorescent instrument lighting was installed for night flying.

With combat reports coming in from Europe in 1941, the Combat Command and Air Materiel Command ordered that all aircraft in production had to incorporate certain items to make them "combat capable". These were self-sealing fuel tanks, no magnesium flares, a low-pressure oxygen system, improved armour protection, and provision for bulletproof glass.

Later all P-38-LO were redesigned to RP-38 to indicate restricted, non-combat status.

The AAF specified that all aircraft with these capabilities be given a "D" suffix. Beginning in August 1941, all production P-38s received the new designation P-38D. Thus, there was no P-38B or P-38C.

Lockheed P-38D Lightning

Because of changes in production, the remainder of the initial order for 66 P-38s was completed as P-38D-LO. The Lockheed designation remained 222-62-02.

The P-38D differed from the P-38 in having a low-pressure oxygen system, self-sealing fuel tanks and provision for flares. Also, there was a change in tailplane incidence, together with a redistribution of elevator mass balances, increased the mechanical advantage of the elevator control. Wing fillets (first installed on the British Model 322) were added during production and then retrofitted to earlier aircraft. These changes resulted in the elimination of buffeting and facilitating dive recovery.

The P-38D had a new low-pressure oxygen system. This system became standard on all subsequent production models. Normal fuel capacity remained 210 gallons, but maximum internal fuel was reduced from 390 to 340 gallons. P-38D did not have retractable landing lights under the wings.

The P-38D and subsequent versions were officially christened "Lightning" by the USAAF.

P-38Ds were not really combat-ready. In 1942, the P-38 was redesignated as RP-38 and the P-38D was redesignated as RP-38D[8].

Lockheed P-38D. Note the national markings with red centre and machine guns mock-ups. (US National Archives)

7   Because there was no model letter, the -LO was included not to be confused with general P-38 designation.

8   The 'R' prefix means 'restricted to non-combat roles'.

P-38D scale plans.
1/72 scale.

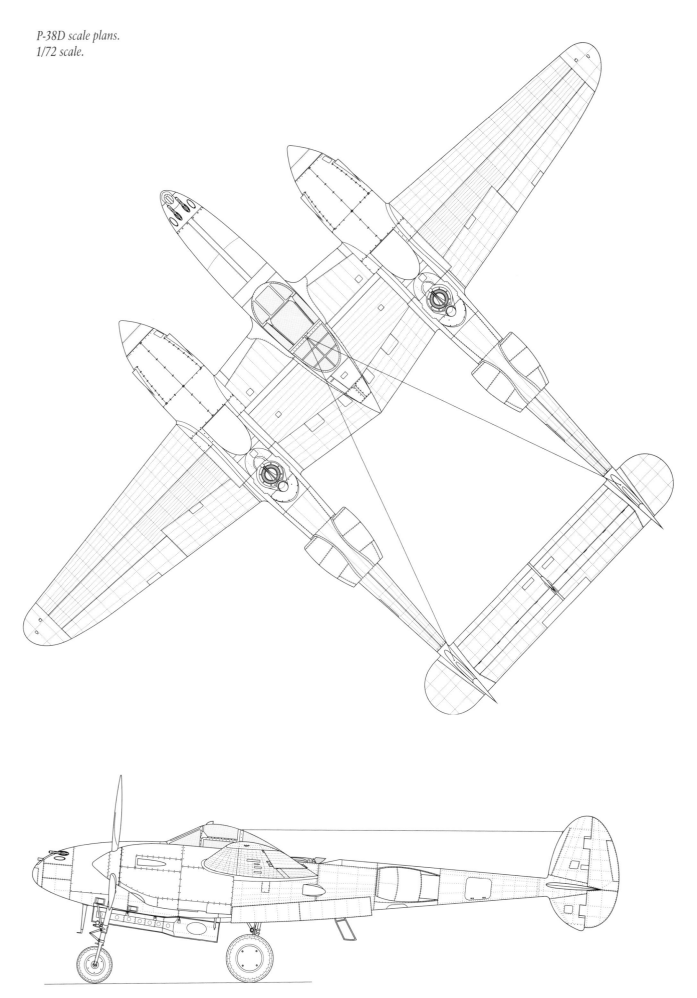

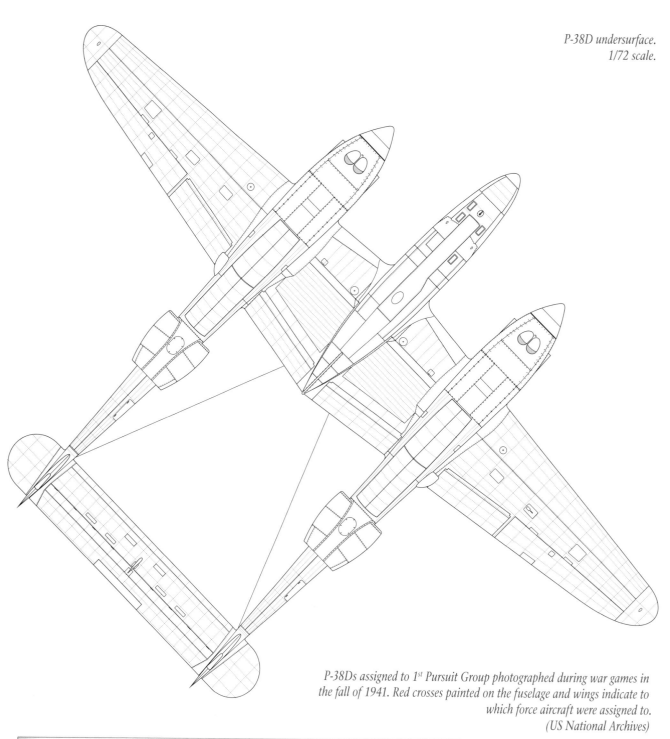

P-38D undersurface.
1/72 scale.

P-38Ds assigned to 1ˢᵗ Pursuit Group photographed during war games in the fall of 1941. Red crosses painted on the fuselage and wings indicate to which force aircraft were assigned to.
(US National Archives)

Lockheed P-38E Lightning

The first production version for the USAAF was the P-38E-LO (company designation Model 222-62-09). It differed from the D-version by incorporating a 20-mm cannon with 150 rounds. The upper engine nacelle air scoop was deleted. The P-38E had improved instrumentation and revised hydraulic and electrical systems. It also had a redesigned nose section with double the ammunition capacity of earlier versions. A new SCR-274N radio was installed. The nose undercarriage was also redesigned. Other changes were new, better flight instruments and a retractable landing light under the port wing.

In the middle of 1941, the Hamilton Standard Hydromatic propellers with hollow steel blades were replaced by Curtiss Electric propellers with dural solid blades.

The P-38E was powered by Allison V-1710-27/29 turbosupercharged engines.

A total of 210 P-38Es were built.

The P-38E was still not yet considered combat-ready, and most P-38Es were redesignated RP-38Es while others were used for various tests.

For example, aircraft serial 41-1983 was used to test several features which later ended up being used in the P-38J and P-38K versions.

Some P-38Es were modified by Lockheed to carry drop tanks as developed for the P-38F-1-LO and later versions.

P-38E serial 41-2239 assigned to the 54th FS during overhaul following a landing accident in which it was seriously damaged on 23 September 1942 at Adak, Aleutian Islands. (US National Archives)

P-38E, s/n unknown, "90", "Pat" of 54th FS. Personal aircraft of Capt. Morgan A. Giffin, commander of the unit. Aleutian Islands. (US National Archives)

P-38Es of 54th FS. Aleutian Islands. (US National Archives)

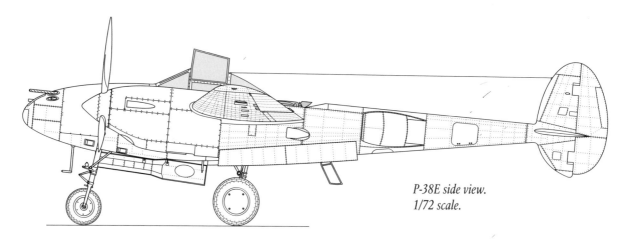

P-38E side view. 1/72 scale.

Two period, colour photos of the early P-38Es before delivery to the units. Aircraft still with older US national markings (with red centre) and no unit markings. (Via Tomasz J. Kopański)

Lockheed F-4 Lightning

99 aircraft originally ordered as P-38Es were finally completed as F-4-1-LO (Model 222-62-13) to be used as unarmed photo reconnaissance aircraft. The F-4 was powered by 1150 hp V-1710-21-29 engines and carried four K-17 cameras in a modified nose. Also during service, these aircraft were modified to carry a pair of 150/165 US gallon drop tanks. Most were retained for training purposes only and then redesigned as RF-4-1-LO.

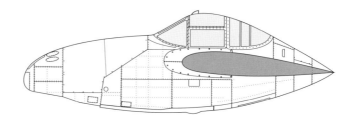

Lockheed F-4 main fuse-lage. 1/72 scale.

Lockheed P-38F Lightning

The P-38F was the first Lightning version that was considered fully combat-ready. This version was introduced in late 1942.

It included 377 US-ordered aircraft, plus 150 planes that had originally been ordered under British and French contracts.

The P-38F was powered by 1325 hp turbosupercharged Allison V-1710-49/53 engines and had the same armament as the E-version. The weight of the P-38F was significantly higher than that of previous versions, so an altitude of 20,000 feet could be reached in 8.8 minutes, a bit slower than the climb rate of earlier versions.

There were five separate production batches of the P-38F, differing from each other mainly in internal equipment.

P-38F-LO (Model 222-60-09).

P-38F with early style canopy. Upper part is opening to the right.

There were some visible changes made to the P-39F as compared to P-38D. The pitot was moved from the nose to the port wing. A SRC-552-A antenna mast was placed under the nose. During production, the canopy was redesigned. The upper section of the canopy could be opened to the rear, not left as before.

128 of the P-38F-LO were built.

P-38F-1-LO (Model 222-60-15), which differed from the P-38F-LO in being modified after delivery, by adding two pylons which could carry a pair of drop tanks or a pair of 1,000-lb bombs under each wing centre sections. Centre section of the wing was strengthened.

This version had SCR-525 and SCR-522 radio.

149 of the P-38F-1-LO were built.

P-38F-5-LO (Model 222-60-12) was built from the onset with provision for drop tanks. It also had revised landing lights, desert equipment, identification lights, and various other minor improvements.

100 of the P-38F-5-LO were built

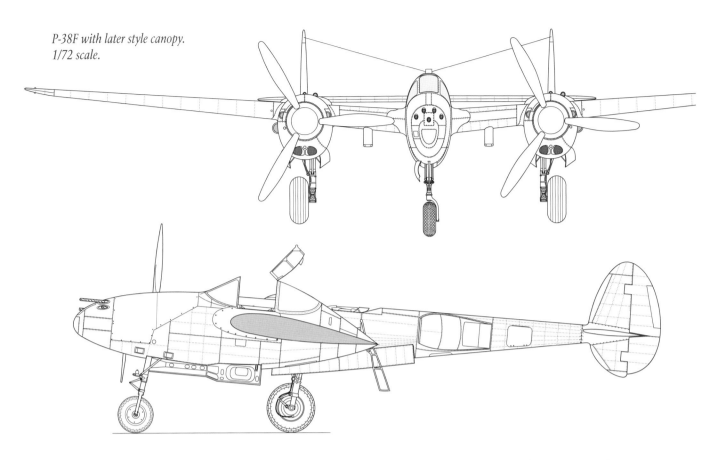

P-38F with later style canopy.
1/72 scale.

P-38F-15-LO, s/n 43-2112, "Sad Sack" assigned to Capt. Ernest K. Osher, commander of the 95th FS, 82nd FG, Berteaux, Algeria. May 1943. (US National Archives)

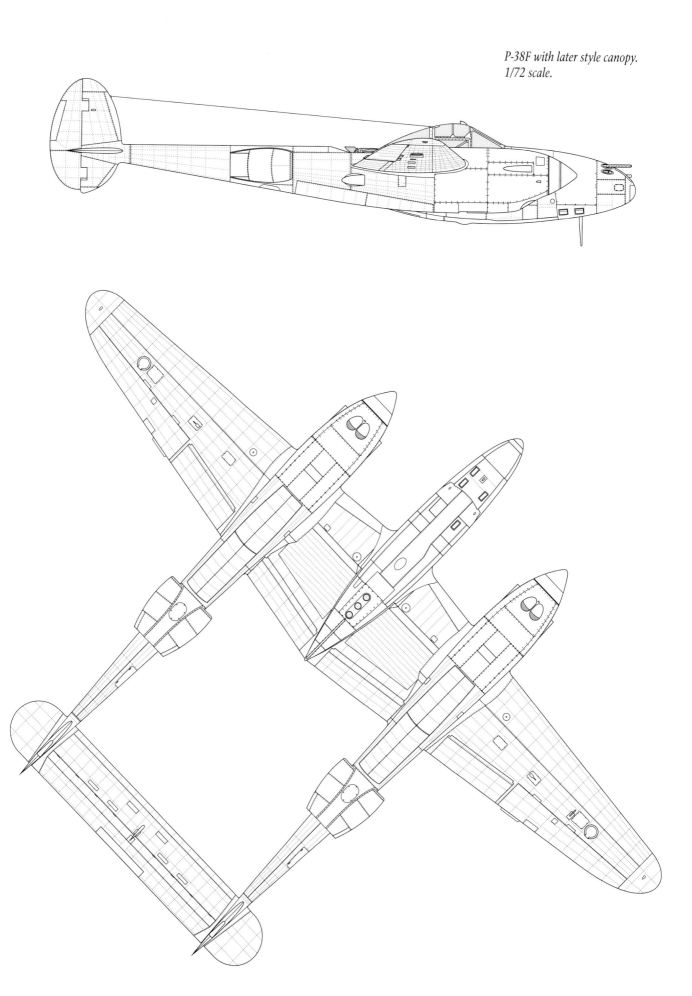

P-38F with later style canopy.
1/72 scale.

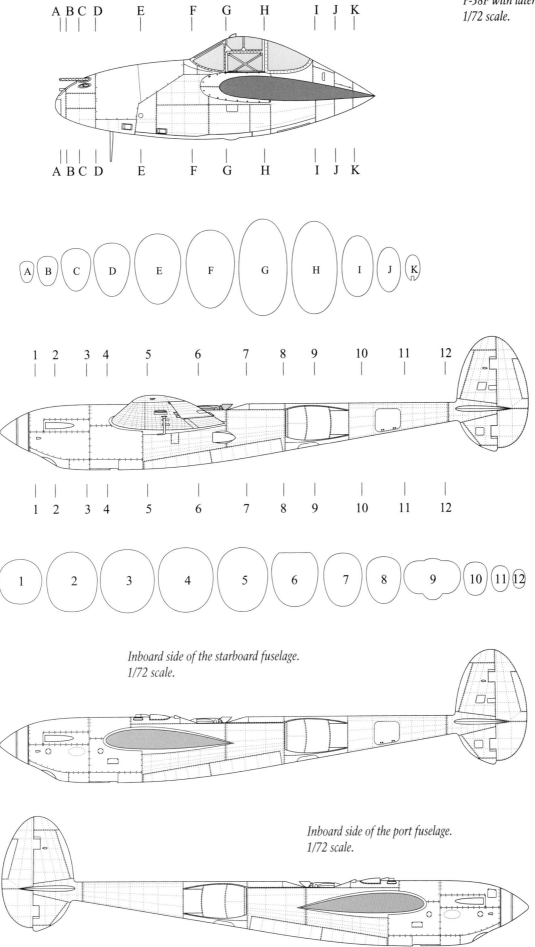

A B C D E F G H I J K

A B C D E F G H I J K

P-38F with later style canopy.
1/72 scale.

A B C D E F G H I J K

1 2 3 4 5 6 7 8 9 10 11 12

1 2 3 4 5 6 7 8 9 10 11 12

1 2 3 4 5 6 7 8 9 10 11 12

Inboard side of the starboard fuselage.
1/72 scale.

Inboard side of the port fuselage.
1/72 scale.

P-38F with later style canopy.
1/72 scale.

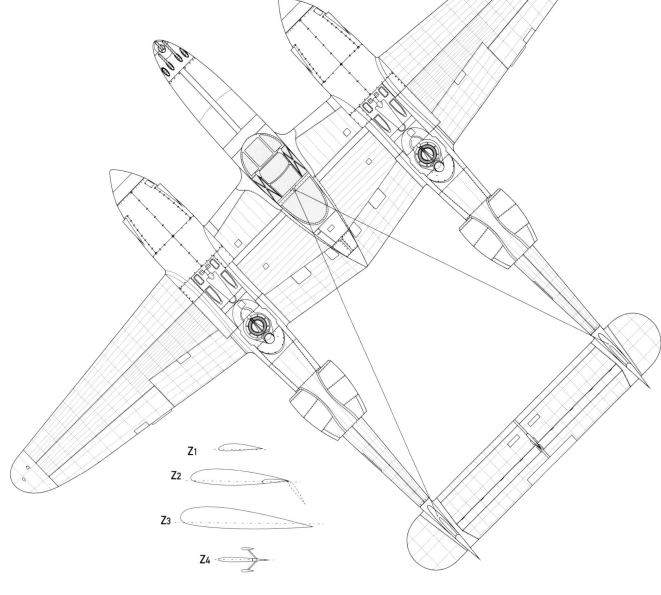

Z_1
Z_2
Z_3
Z_4

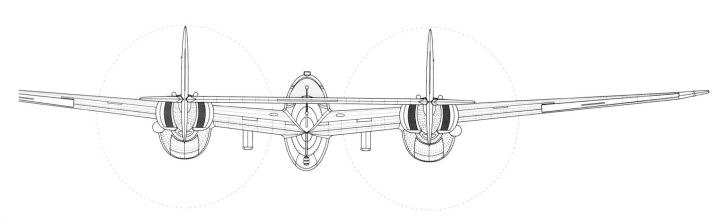

Above: Shark-mouthed P-38Fs of the 39th FS, 35th FG. Jackson airfield Port Moresby.

Below: P-38F-5-LO, s/n 43-12596 of 2nd Service Group at Camp Tripoli, Island. Winter 1942/43.

(Both US National Archives)

The 29 **P-38F-13-LOs** and the 212 **P-38F-15-LOs** were ex-British contract aircraft and were designated Model 322-60-19s by the company. The P-38F-13-LO had modified instruments meeting the British Approved Specification No. 2338.

The P-38F-15-LO introduced combat flaps which could be rapidly extended to 8 degrees during manoeuvres to tighten the turning radius. Fixed tabs were added to the trailing edge of each aileron. The landing light was added to the starboard wing. Three identification lights were added under the aft central fuselage.

Lockheed F-4A-1-LO Lightning

Twenty P-38F-1-LO airframes with 1325 hp V-1710-49/53 engines were completed as F-4A-1-LO (Model 222-60-13).

F-4A-1-LO scale plans. 1/72 scale. They were unarmed photo-reconnaissance aircraft with four K-17 cameras in a redesigned nose.

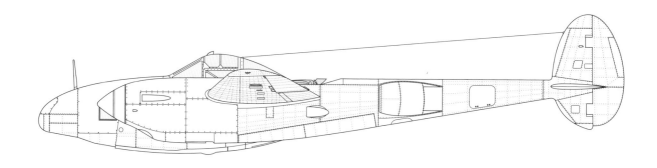

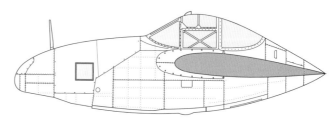

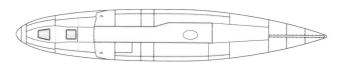

Camera mounted in the F-4A nose. (US National Archives)

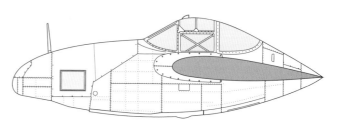

Different version of the port side camera window. 1/72 scale.

Above: Crew repairing and servicing a F-4A at the air base somewhere in India.

Below: F-4A of the 9th Photographic Reconnaissance Squadron landing at an air base in Dum Dum, India, March 1943.

(Both US National Archives)

Lockheed P-38G Lightning

Production of the P-38G (Model 222-68-12) began in June of 1942. It was basically similar to the P-38F apart from a change to the Allison V-1710-51/55 (F10) engine with increased boost ratings and offering 1325 hp for take-off. However, the engine was limited to 1150 hp at 27,000 feet due to inadequate cooling.

Also, the P-38G carried a new SCR-274N radio and A-9 oxygen equipment.

There were six production blocks.

P-38G-1-LO which were generally similar to the P-38F-15-LOs but with the new engines, improved oxygen equipment and new radios.

80 of the P-38G-1-LO were built.

P-38G-3-LO with B-13 superchargers.

12 were built.

P-38G-5-LO with revised instrumentation.

68 were built.

P-38G-10-LO which combined the improvements introduced in the two previous blocks with winterization equipment, provision for carrying 1,600 lb bombs underneath the wing centre section, or a triple cluster of 4.5-inch rocket launchers on each side of the central nacelle.

548 were built.

The 374 aircraft of Model 322-68-19s (174 **P-38G-13-LOs**, equivalent to the P-38G-3-LO and 200 **P-38G-15-LOs**, corresponding to the P-38G-5-LO) came from the cancelled British contract for Lightning IIs which was taken over by the USAAF. (*See Lightning I and Lightning II*)

P-38G-15-LO, s/n 43-25xx of 49th FS, 14th FG. Aircraft assigned to Capt. Lloyd K. DeMoss. (US National Archives)

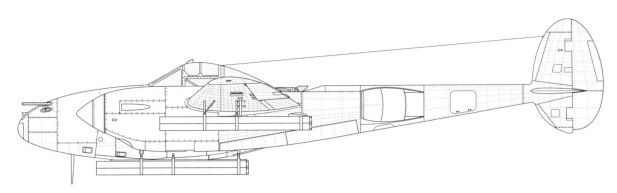

Above: P-38G with bazooka launchers. 1/72 scale.

Left: P-38G-13-LO, s/n 43-2308 "Shoot. You're Faded" assigned to 2nd Lt John A. MacKay of 27th FS, 1st FG.

P-38G, s/n 43-2295 fitted with M8 4.5 inch 'bazooka' type rocket launchers photographed at Eglin Field's armament test centre. The only combat unit of record to utilize the installation was the 459th FS in the China-Burma-India theatre. *(Both US National Archives)*

29

*P-38G-15-LO
s/n 43-2427 of the 71ˢᵗ
FS, 1ˢᵗ FG. North Africa,
April 1943.
(US National Archives)*

*P-38G-10-LO,
s/n 42-13437, "Golden
Eagle" of the 459ᵗʰ FS,
51ˢᵗ FG. It was the oldest
operational "Lightning"
in the Squadron.
(US National Archives)*

Lockheed F-5A Lightning

This was an unarmed photographic reconnaissance versions of the P-38G. It could carry five cameras. A single **F-5A-2-LO** (model 222-62-16) was completed by modifying a P-38E airframe (41-2157) by installing V-1719-21/29 engines. The rest of the F-5As (Model 222-68-16) had P-38G airframes and 1325 hp V-1710-51/55 engines.

Twenty **F-5A-1-LO**s, 20 **F-5A-3-LO**s, and 140 **F-5A-10-LO**s had the same modifications as P-38G versions with corresponding block numbers, and came off the production line in parallel with their fighter counterparts.

Additionally, one F-5A-10-LO (s/n 42-12975) was modified as an experimental two-seat reconnaissance aircraft under the designation XF-5D-LO. The camera operator was located in a glazed nose with two forward-firing 0.50-in machine guns. Three K-17 cameras were installed, one underneath the nose and one in each tail boom.

F-5A main fuselage plans. 1/72 scale.

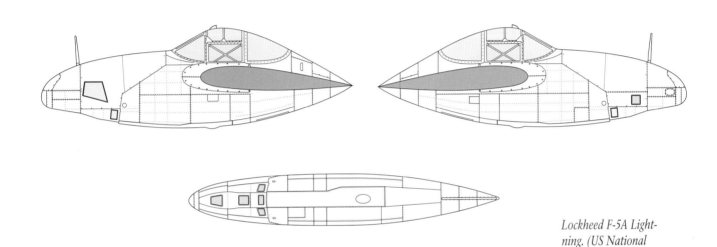

Lockheed F-5A Lightning. (US National Archives)

Standard P-38 (fighter version) main fuselage.

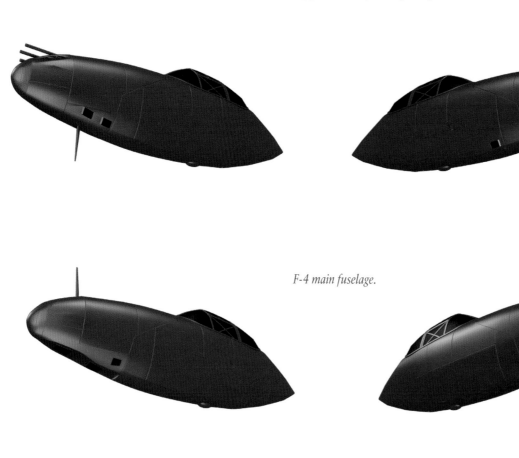

F-4 main fuselage.

F-4A main fuselage.

F-5A main fuselage.

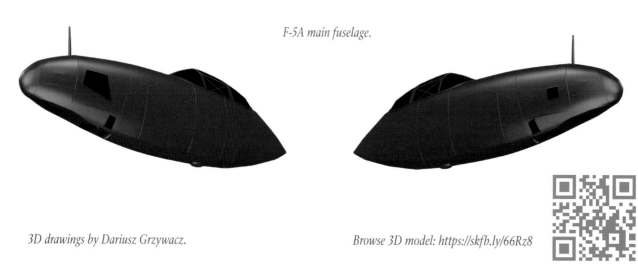

3D drawings by Dariusz Grzywacz.

Browse 3D model: https://skfb.ly/66Rz8

F-5A taking off for the mission, North Africa.
(US National Archives)

Lockheed P-38H Lightning

The P-38H (Model 222-81-20) was powered by 1425 hp Allison V-1710-89/91 engines. Also, the P-38H was fitted with automatic oil radiator flaps in order to solve an engine overheating problem and enable military power above 25,000 feet to be increased from 1150 to 1240 hp. An M-2C cannon took the place of the M-1, and the bomb capacity for each under-wing rack was raised to 1600 pounds. In most other respects, this model was identical to the P-38G-10-LO.

226 **P-38H-1-LO** were built.

P-38H side views. **P-38H-5-LO** was fitted with B-33 instead of B-13 turbosuperchargers.
1/72 scale. 375 were built.

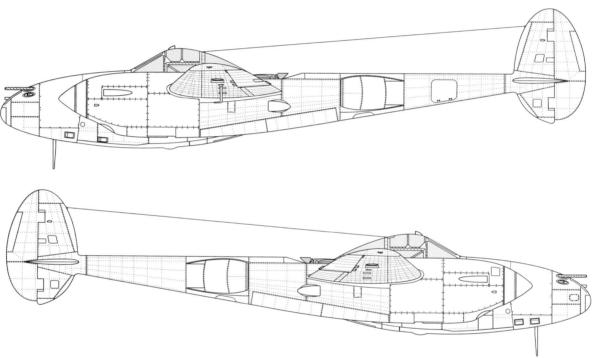

P-38H-5-LO, s/n 42-67026, (c/n 422-1537), CL-P of the 338th FS, 55th FG. Aircraft assigned to Chester A. "Chet" Patterson. (US National Archives)

P-38 H main fuselage. Note the additional access panel on the nose, seen in the many P-38H photos. 1/72 scale.

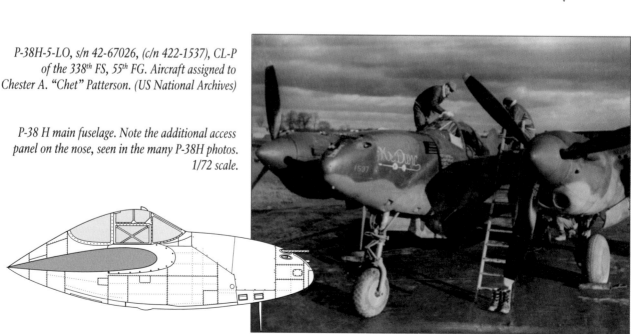

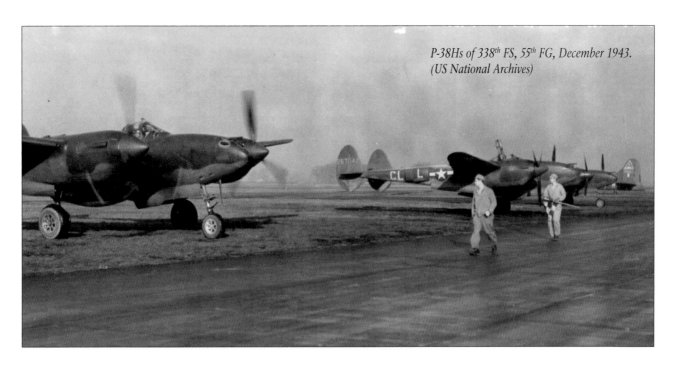

P-38Hs of 338th FS, 55th FG, December 1943.
(US National Archives)

P-38H-5-LO, s/n 42-67074, CG-J, "Texas Ranger" of 38th FS, 55th FG.
(US National Archives)

P-38H, s/c 42-66718, CY-T, 338th FS, 55th FG.
(US National Archives)

P-38H-1-LO, s/n 42-66717 of 449ᵗʰ FS, 51ˢᵗ FG, Kunming, China. (US National Archives)

Lockheed XP-38A Lightning

The Army also ordered completion of one P-38-LO (s/n 40-762) equipped with a pressurized cockpit. Aircraft was redesignated XP-38A. To offset the extra weight of the pressurized cockpit, the 37-mm cannon was to be replaced by a 20-mm unit, but no armament was fitted to XP-38A prototype. Manufacturer's trials were performed between May and December of 1942, and the XP-38A was accepted by the USAAF at the end of that year.

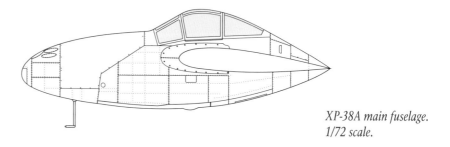

XP-38A main fuselage.
1/72 scale.

Lockheed P-38 serials

Version	Lockheed Model	Contract Number	Delivered Qty	Lockheed production number	Serials
XP-38	022-64-01	AC-9974	1	2201	37-457
YP-38	122-62-02	AC-12523	13	2202 - 2214	39-689 to 39-701
P-38/RP-38	222-62-08	AC-13205	18	2215 - 2232	40-744 to 40-761
			11	2234 - 2244	40-763 to 40-773
P-38D/RP-38D	222-62-08D	AC-13205 C.0.3377	36	2245 - 2280	40-774 to 40-809
XP-38A	622-62-10	AC-13205 C.O.8	1	2233	40-762
XP-49	522-66-07	AC-13476	1		40-3055
P-38E/RP-38E	222-62-09	AC-15646	115	5201 - 5315	41-1983 to 41-2097
			21	5318 - 5338	41-2100 to 41-2120
			1	5390	41-2172
			1	5437	41-2219
			72	5439 - 5510	41-2221 to 41-2292
F-4-1-LO	222-62-13	AC-15646 CO. 11	2	5316 - 5317	41-2098 to 41-2099
			36	5339 - 5374	41-2121 to 42-2156
			14	5376 - 5389	41-2158 to 41-2171
			46	5391 - 5436	41-2173 41-2218
			1	5438	41-2220
F-5A-2-LO	222-62-16	AC-15646	1	5375	41-2157
P-38F	222-60-09	AC-15646	29	5511 - 5539	41-2293 to 41-2321
			36	5541 - 5576	41-2323 to 41-2358
			4	5601 - 5604	41-2383 to 41-2386
			5	5606 - 5610	41-2388 to 41-2392
			11	5613 - 5623	41-7486 to 41-7496
			16	5625 - 5640	41-7498 to 41-7513
			9	5643 - 5651	41-7516 to 41-7524
			5	5653 - 5657	41-7526 to 41-7530
			3	5659 - 5661	41-7532 to 41-7534
			3	5663 - 5665	41-7536 to 41-7538
			2	5669 - 5670	41-7542 to 41-7543
			1	5672	41-7545
			1	5674	41-7547
			1	5678	41-7551
F-4A-1-LO	222-60-13	AC-15646	20	5580 - 5599	41-2362 to 41-2381
P-38F-1-LO	222-60-15	AC-15646	1	5540	41-2322
			3	5577 - 5579	41-2359 to 41-2361
			1	5612 -	41-7485
			1	5624 -	41-7497
			2	5641 - 5642	41-7514 to 41-7515

			1	5652 -	41-7525
			1	5658 -	41-7531
			1	5662 -	41-7535
P-38F-1-LO	222-60-15	AC-15646	3	5666 - 5668	41-7539 to 41-7541
			1	5671 -	41-7544
			1	5673 -	41-7546
			3	5675 - 5677	41-7548 to 41-7550
			129	5679 - 5807	41-7552 to 41-7680
P-38F-1-LO	222-60-12	AC-15646	1	5600	41-2382
			1	5605 -	41-2387
			1	5611 -	41-7484
P-38F-5-LO	222-60-12	AC-21217	100	7001 - 7100	42-12567 to 42-12666
P-38G-1-LO	222-68-12	AC-21217	80	7121 - 7200	42-12687 to 42-12766
P-38G-3-LO	222-68-12	AC-21217	12	7221 - 7232	42-12787 to 42-12798
P-38G-5-LO	222-68-12	AC-21217	68	7233 - 7300	42-12799 to 42-12866
P-38G-10-LO	222-68-12	AC-21217	97	7304 - 7400	42-12870 to 42-12966
			80	7421 - 7500	42-12987 to 42-13066
			140	7561 - 7700	42-13127 to 42-13266
			231	7761 - 7991	42-13327 to 42-13557
F-5A-1-LO	222-68-16	AC-21217	20	7101 -7120	42-12667 to 42-12686
F-5A-3-LO	222-68-16	AC-21217	20	7201 - 7220	42-12767 to 42-12786
F-5A-10-LO	222-68-16	AC-21217	20	7401 - 7420	42-12967 to 42-12986
			60	7501 - 7560	42-13067 to 42-13126
			60	7701 - 7760	42-13267 to 42-13326
322-F	322-61-03	A-242	0		France collapsed in June 1940
322-B	322-61-04	BR-A-242/AC-31707	3	3001 - 3003	AE 978 to AE 980
P-322-I	322-61-04	BR-A-242/AC-31707	19	3004 - 3022	AE 981 to AE 999
P-322-I	322-62-18	BR-A-242/AC-31707	121	3023 - 3143	AF 100 to AF220
P-38F-13-LO	322-60-19	A-242/AC-31707	29	3144 - 3172	43-2035 to 43-2063
P-38F-15-LO	322-60-19	A-242/AC-31707	121	3173 - 3293	43-2064 to 43-2184
P-38G-13-LO	322-68-19	A-242/AC-31707	174	3294 - 3467	43-2185 to 43-2358
P-38G-15-LO	322-68-19	A-242/AC-31707	33	3468 - 3500	43-2359 to 43-2391
P-38G-15-LO	322-68-19	A-242/AC-31707	167	3502 - 3668	43-2392 to 43-2558
P-38H-1-LO	422-81-20	AC-21217	1	1005 -	42-13559
P-38H-1-LO	422-81-20	AC-24636	225	1013 - 1237	42-66502 to 42-66726
P-38H-5-LO	422-81-20	AC-24636	375	1238 - 1612	42-66727 to 42-67101

Continue reading on P-38 later versions in the book:
Lockheed P-38 J-L Lightning,
ISBN: 978-83-61421-69-6.

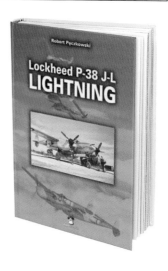

Technical description of P-38H

Single-seat, twin-engined, cantilever mid-wing monoplane of all-metal construction with retractable undercarriage, designed in a twin-boom layout with a central fuselage pod that housed the cockpit and armament.

The central fuselage of semi-monocoque design with oval cross-section, with smooth duralumin covering. The skin thickness was between 0.025" (0.64 mm) and 0.051" (1.3 mm). The nose section housed the built-in armament and ammunition boxes. Access to it was provided by upward-opening covers on both sides of the fuselage. A VHF antenna was attached at the bottom nose covering. The pilot's cockpit was located aft of the frame that separated the armament compartment. The heavily glazed cockpit canopy (its profile merged in with the wing trailing edge) provided rearward visibility.

The cockpit canopy was of three-section design. The front and rear sections were fixed, while the top of the central section opened upwards and backwards, hinged on the duralumin reinforcement aft of the pilot's seat, and it could be jettisoned in emergency.

Side panels could be lowered using hand cranks. The windscreen included a bullet-proof glass panel at the front. It was bonded with vinyl adhesive from five layers of glass. Side panels of the canopy were made from twin layers of glass bonded with the same adhesive. A ladder was fitted for entry into the cockpit and it retracted into the lower part of the pod. The nose wheel leg was fitted in the forward nose, attached on a special joint to the diagonal reinforced frame that separated the armament compartment from the cockpit. When retracted the nose wheel was located under the cockpit floor.

The cockpit was armour-protected and was fitted with a full set of flying and navigation instruments that allowed flying in adverse weather. The engine, propeller and undercarriage panel was located on the port side. The flap lever and radio panels were located on the starboard side.

The radio blocks were located on a shelf aft of the pilot's seat, immediately below the transparent hood. The rudder pedal bar was fitted in the floor, below the instrument panel, with adjustment of distance from the pilot's seat. Undercarriage brake levers were mounted in the rudder pedals. The yoke was attached to a control column that was pivoted under the floor on the starboard side. The pilot's seat, pressed from a laminate, included a recess for the parachute. Its back section included a 0.375" (ca. 9.5 mm) armour plate of hardened steel. Pilot's head was protected by a plate of similar material.

Identification lights were fitted in the bottom of the fuselage on the centreline.

The three-piece wing, cantilever, two-spar, all-metal, was of tapered planform with rounded tips, covered with smooth duralumin covering, its thickness ranging between 0.020" (ca. 0.5 mm) and 0.040" (ca. 1 mm). The wing tips were highly flattened on the underside. The wing airfoil was NACA 23016 at the root (aircraft centreline) changing to NACA 4412 at wing tips. The wing centre section was an integral structure with the cockpit and the engine nacelles. Outer wing panels were attached to the centre section at the wing-engine nacelle joint.

Metal ailerons, covered with smooth duralumin, deflected differentially with hydraulic actuation. Four weights were attached to the aileron spar for mass balance. The design of the aileron attachment was rarely seen on other combat aircraft: the aileron was attached to the upper wing surface on a piano hinge along its entire span. Each aileron was fitted with a balance tab adjusted on the ground and a trim tab adjustable in flight (the latter were deleted on later variants).

Fowler flaps of metal construction covered the wing span from the pilot's pod to the ailerons, with a break for the engine booms.

Four integral self-sealing fuel tanks with a total capacity of 1,136 litres (in later versions) were fitted inside the wing centre section.

A night landing light was fitted in the leading edge of the port wing. Navigation lights were fitted on the upper and lower wing tip surfaces.

Attachments for external stores (bombs, torpedoes) or fuel tanks were located symmetrically under the wing centre section. The pitot tube was located under the port wing.

Tail: cantilever, of all-metal construction, with smooth duralumin covering.

Three-piece horizontal tail, with rectangular planform with semi-circular tips extending beyond the engine booms. Single-piece elevator, mass balanced, fitted with a balance tab adjustable in flight from the cockpit.

Twin vertical tail surfaces, with characteristic oval planform. The shape of the section above the tail boom was an ogival ellipse, while the section below the tail boom was semi-circular with a small steel skid protruding. The fin, split in the same way as the rudder, consisted of the upper section (above the boom) and the bottom section (below the boom). Aerodynamically balanced rudders were fitted with balance tabs adjustable in flight. White navigation lights were fitted on outboard sides of the fins.

Rudders, elevator, ailerons and trim tabs were controlled by steel cables.

Tricycle undercarriage, completely retractable and faired over in flight with covers that completed the outer streamlined form of the fuselage and booms. Main wheels were retractable backwards into the engine booms, and the nose wheel into the pilot's pod. The nose wheel was fitted with a vibration damper. The oleo legs were hydraulically retracted and lowered. The main wheels were fitted with drum brakes and a parking brake.

Power plant consisted of two Allison V-1710-89/-91 liquid-cooled 12-cylinder Vee in-line engines, with cylinder rows banked at 60°, with various engine variants depending on the version of the aircraft.

Cylinder diameter was 5.5 inch (139.7 mm), piston stroke was 6 inch (152.4 mm). Cubic capacity was 1,710 cu. in. (28 litres), compression ratio 6.65:1.

Engine specification Allison V-1710-89/91 (F-17R/L)	
Fuel	100/130-octane
Take-off power	1,425 hp at 3,000 rpm (but was limited to 1,240 hp due to cooling problems
Normal power @ altitude	1,100 hp at 2,600 rpm @ 30,000 ft (9.150 m)
Combat power (15-minute) @ altitude	1,425 hp at 3000 rpm @ 30,000 ft (9.150 m)
Empty engine weight	1,395 lbs (633.5 kg)
Dimensions: length, height, width	85.91" (2.180 m), 36.65" (0.958 m), 29.28" (0.744 m)

Armament of the aircraft consisted of a single 20 mm AN-M-Z cannon and four 0.5 in. (12.7 mm) M-2 machine guns. The machine gun positions were staggered to allow a greater amount of ammunition. Bigger ammunition boxes could be located one behind another rather than in pairs side-by-side. Normal ammunition load was 300 rounds per gun, but a maximum of 500 rounds per gun could be loaded into each box.

The aircraft could carry a maximum load of 1,450 kg bombs on carriers under the wing centre section. There were other modifications that allowed the P-38 to carry three-tube Bazooka launchers.

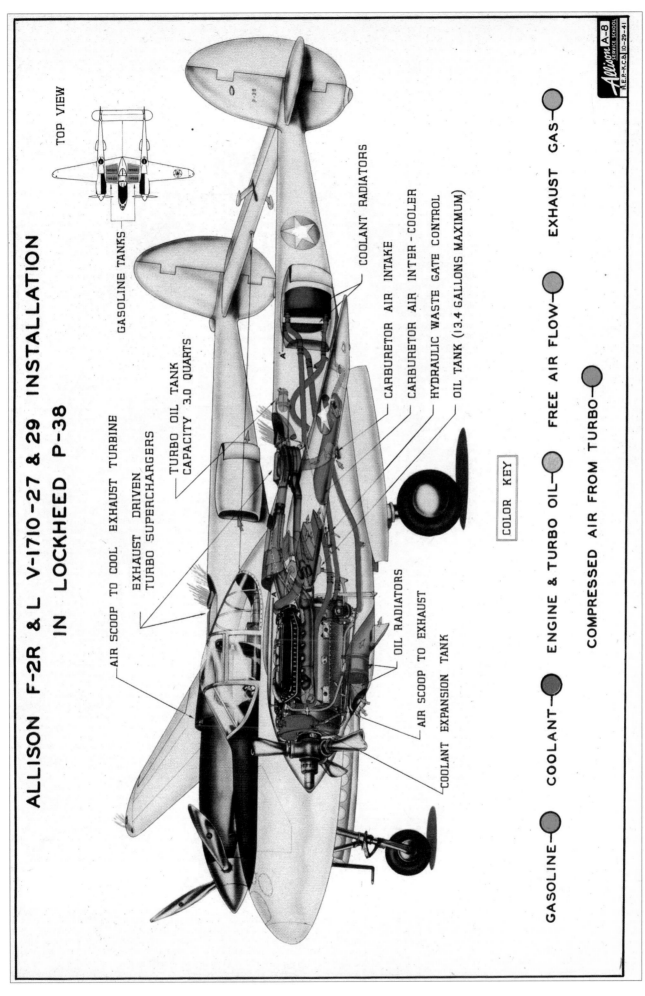

ALLISON F-2R & L V-1710-27 & 29 INSTALLATION
IN LOCKHEED P-38

TOP VIEW

GASOLINE TANKS

AIR SCOOP TO COOL EXHAUST TURBINE

EXHAUST DRIVEN
TURBO SUPERCHARGERS

TURBO OIL TANK
CAPACITY 3.0 QUARTS

COOLANT RADIATORS

CARBURETOR AIR INTAKE

CARBURETOR AIR INTER-COOLER

HYDRAULIC WASTE GATE CONTROL

OIL TANK (13.4 GALLONS MAXIMUM)

AIR SCOOP TO EXHAUST

OIL RADIATORS

COOLANT EXPANSION TANK

COLOR KEY

GASOLINE

COOLANT

ENGINE & TURBO OIL

FREE AIR FLOW

EXHAUST GAS

COMPRESSED AIR FROM TURBO

Allison A-8
SERVICE SCHOOL
A.E.P.-K.C.b 10-29-41

P-38 Specifications

	XP-38	YP-38	British Lightning Mk. I	P-38-LO	P-38D	P-38E	P-38F	P-38G & F-5A	P-38H
Dimensions									
Length:	37 ft 10 in (11.53 m)								
Wingspan:	52 ft 0 in (15.85 m)								
Height:	12 ft 10 in (3.91 m)								
Wing area:	327.5 ft² (30.43 m²)								
Airfoil:	NACA 23016 / NACA 4412								
Powerplants	Allison V-1710-11/-15, C-9	Allison V-1710-27/-29, F-2	Allison V-1710-15, C-15	Allison V-1710-27/-29, F-2	Allison V-1710-27/-29, F-2	Allison V-1710-27/-29, F-4	Allison V-1710-49/-53, F-5	Allison V-1710-51/-55, F-10	Allison V-1710-89/-91, F-17
Horspower (each)	1,150 hp	1,150 hp	1,090 hp	1,150 hp	1,150 hp	1,150 hp	1,325 hp	1,325 hp	1,425 hp limited to 1,240 due to cooling problem
Max speed	413 mph at 20,000 feet	405 mph at 20,000 feet	357 mph	395 mph at 20,000 feet	390 mph at 20,000 feet	395 mph at 20,000 feet	395 mph at 25,000 feet	400 mph at 25,000 feet	402 mph at 25,000 feet
Cruising speed	330 mph	330 mph		310 mph	300 mph	300 mph	305 mph	340 mph	250 mph
Rate of climb	6.5 minutes to 20,000 feet	6.0 minutes to 20,000 feet			8.0 minutes to 20,000 feet	8.0 minutes to 20,000 feet	8.8 minutes to 20,000 feet	8.5 minutes to 20,000 feet	6.5 minutes to 20,000 feet
Ceiling	38,000 feet	38,000 feet	40,000 feet		39,000 feet	39,000 feet	39,000 feet	39,000 feet	40,000 feet
Maximum range	1,390 miles	1,150 miles	1,150 miles	1,490 miles	970 miles	975 miles	1,925 miles	2,400 miles	2,400 miles
Empty weight:	11,507 lb	11,171 lb	11,945 lb	11,672 lb	11,780 lb	11,880 lb	12,264 lb	12,200 lb	12,380 lb
Loaded weight:	13,964 lb	13,500 lb	14,467 lb	14,178 lb	14,456 lb	14,424 lb	15,900 lb	15,800 lb	16,300 lb
Max. take off weight:	15,416 lb	14,248 lb		15,340 lb	15,548 lb	15,482 lb	18,000 lb	19,800 lb	20,300 lb

P-38 comparison

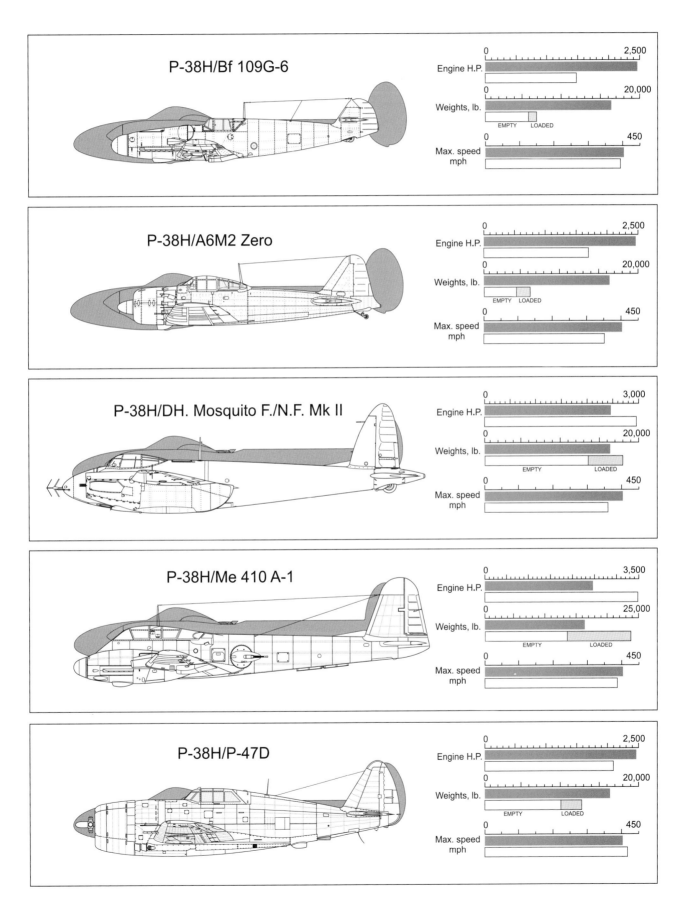

P-38H/Bf 109G-6

Engine H.P.	0 — 2,500
Weights, lb.	0 — 20,000 (EMPTY / LOADED)
Max. speed mph	0 — 450

P-38H/A6M2 Zero

Engine H.P.	0 — 2,500
Weights, lb.	0 — 20,000 (EMPTY / LOADED)
Max. speed mph	0 — 450

P-38H/DH. Mosquito F./N.F. Mk II

Engine H.P.	0 — 3,000
Weights, lb.	0 — 20,000 (EMPTY / LOADED)
Max. speed mph	0 — 450

P-38H/Me 410 A-1

Engine H.P.	0 — 3,500
Weights, lb.	0 — 25,000 (EMPTY / LOADED)
Max. speed mph	0 — 450

P-38H/P-47D

Engine H.P.	0 — 2,500
Weights, lb.	0 — 20,000 (EMPTY / LOADED)
Max. speed mph	0 — 450

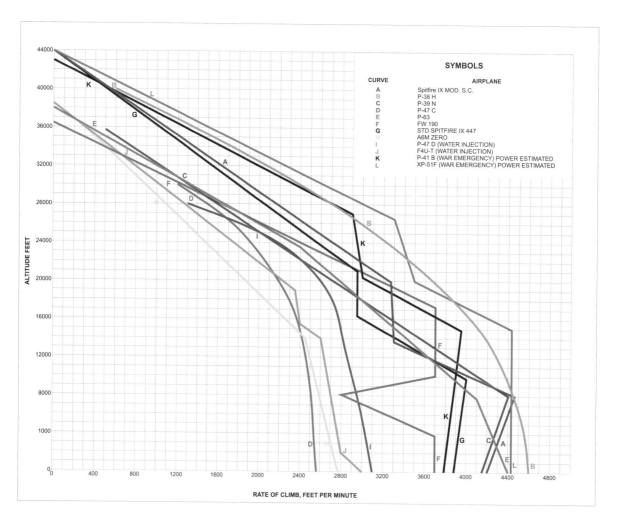

SYMBOLS

CURVE	AIRPLANE
A	Spitfire IX MOD. S.C.
B	P-38 H
C	P-39 N
D	P-47 C
E	P-63
F	FW 190
G	STD SPITFIRE IX 447
H	A6M ZERO
I	P-47 D (WATER INJECTION)
J	F4U-T (WATER INJECTION)
K	P-41 B (WAR EMERGENCY) POWER ESTIMATED
L	XP-51F (WAR EMERGENCY) POWER ESTIMATED

RATE OF CLIMB, FEET PER MINUTE

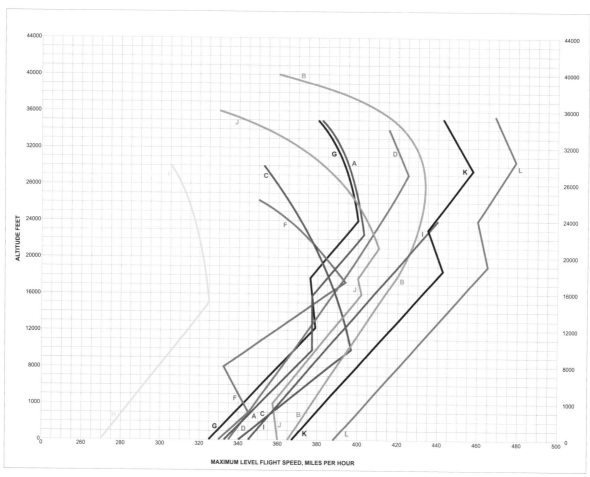

MAXIMUM LEVEL FLIGHT SPEED, MILES PER HOUR

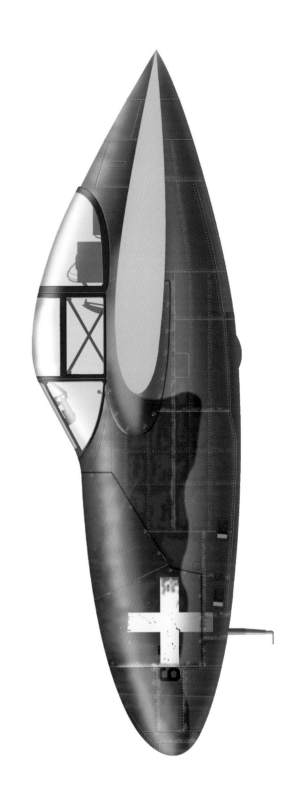

P-38D, (69 1P) of 1st Pursuit Group (PG), late 1941 during the Army's Carolina Manoeuvres, a series of war games held in late 1941. Aircraft Olive Drab (OD) uppersurfaces with Neutral Grey (NG) undersurfaces. Red spinners. White crosses indicate aircraft assignment to the "White Force" during the manoeuvres. US National Insignia as used till May 1941 in four positions.

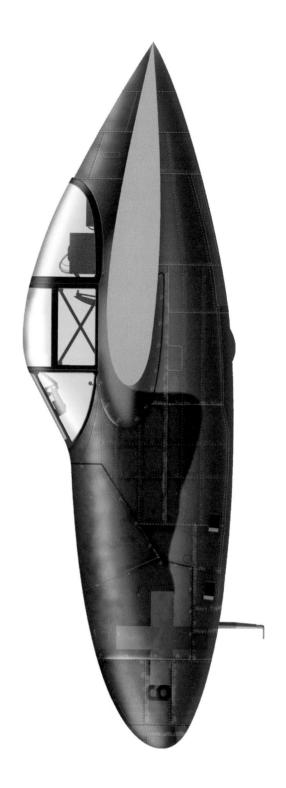

P-38D, (67 1P) of 1st PG, late 1941 during the Army's Carolina Manoeuvres, a series of war games held in late 1941. Aircraft OD uppersurfaces with NG undersurfaces. OD spinners. Red crosses indicate aircraft assignment to the "Red Force" during the manoeuvres. US National Insignia as used till May 1941 in four positions.

Above: P-38D, (54 1P) of 1st PG, late 1941 during the Army's Carolina Manoeuvres, a series of war games held in late 1941. Aircraft OD uppersurfaces with NG undersurfaces. OD spinners. White crosses indicate aircraft assignment to the "White Force" during the manoeuvres. US National Insignia as used till May 1941 in four positions.
Below: P-38E shown before delivery to the unit. Aircraft OD uppersurfaces with NG undersurfaces. OD spinners. US National Insignia as used till May 1941 in four positions.

Above: P-38F-5-LO, s/n 42-12xxx, "33"/S of 347ᵗʰ FS, 350ᵗʰ FG, 13ᵗʰ AF. Guadalcanal, February 1943. Aircraft OD uppersurfaces with NG under-surfaces. OD spinners. US National Insignia used between May 1942 and June 1943 in four positions.

Below: P-38F, s/n 41-7498, UN-G of 94ᵗʰ FS, 1ˢᵗ FG, 12ⁿᵈ AF. North Africa, early 1943. Aircraft OD uppersurfaces with NG undersurfaces. OD spinners. US National Insignia with yellow border (used during Operation Torch) in four positions.

Above: P-38F-5-LO, s/n 42-12653, "27" of 39th FS, 35th FG 5th Air Force. Assigned to Captain Charlie King. On 8 January 1943, took off from 14 Mile Drome (Schwimmer) piloted by Richard I. Bong on escort mission no. 1 over Lae. During the air combat, Bong claimed his fifth aerial victory. Aircraft OD uppersurfaces with NG undersurfaces. Blue spinners. US National Insignia used between May 1942 and June 1943 in four positions.

Portrait of Richard I. Bong. (Drawing Zbigniew Kolacha)

Above: F-4 Lightning, s/n 41-2130. Of 8th PRS, originally as "Malaria Mabel" with squadron number "30". Aircraft stripped of its Haze Paint photographed at Fourteen Mile Strip on 22 October 1943. By this time the aircraft was used as a squadron hack. US National Insignia with only white bars.

Below: P-38F, formerly of 71st FS, 1st FG wrongly landed at Sardinia on 12 June 1943. Later used by col. Angelo Tondi commander of 1º Reparto-Aeromoboli Terrestri, 1º Centro Sperimentale at Gudonia, 1943. On 11 August 1943, Tondi took off to intercept a formation of about 50 bombers, returning from the bombing of Terni (Umbria). Tondi attacked B-17G, s/n 42-30307, "Bonny Sue". Aircraft fell off the shore of Torvaianica, near Rome. Aircraft OD uppersurfaces with NG undersurfaces with overpainted American markings. White spinners.

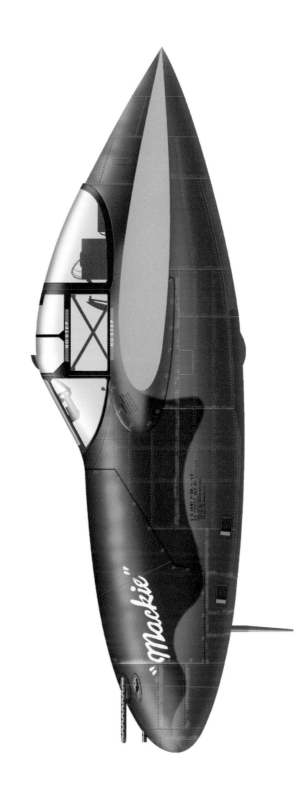

P-38G-10-LO, s/n 42-12926, "10", "Mackie" of 82nd FS, 78th FG, early 1943, before transfer to North Africa. Personal aircraft of Capt. Harry J Dayhuff. Aircraft OD uppersurfaces with NG undersurfaces. White spinners. Note that the year "2" is missing from the serial number on the tail. US National Insignia with yellow border (used during Operation Torch) in 4 positions.

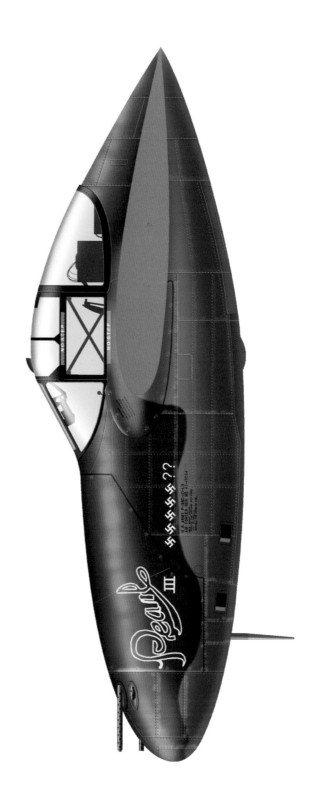

P-38G-10-LO, s/n 42-13054, BS, "Pearl III" of 96th FS, 82nd FG, May 1943. Personal aircraft of 1st Lt. Charles Zubarik. Aircraft OD uppersurfaces with NG undersurfaces. Red spinners. US National Insignia with yellow border (used during Operation Torch) in 4 positions.

P-38G-13-LO, s/n 43-2264, "147", "Miss Virginia" of 339th FS, 347th FG, 13th AF. Guadalcanal, early 1943. Aircraft assigned to Lt. Robert Petit. Aircraft OD uppersurfaces with NG undersurfaces. US National Insignia red between May 1942 and June 1943 in four positions.

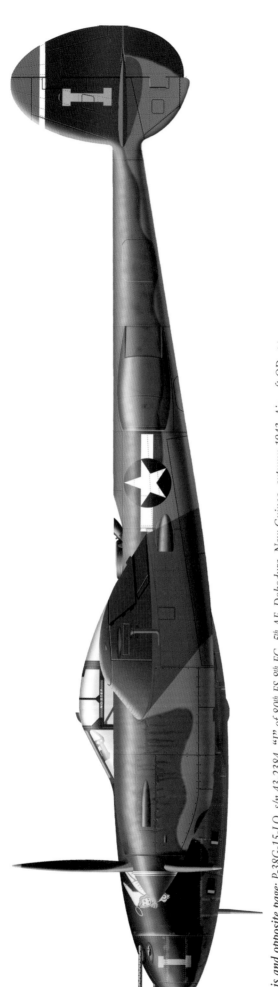

This and opposite page: P-38G-15-LO, s/n 43-2384, "I" of 80th FS 8th FG, 5th AF, Dobodura, New Guinea, autumn 1943. Aircraft OD upper-surfaces with NG undersurfaces. Green spinners. US National Insignia red between May 1942 and June 1943 in four positions. Note added white bars to the insignia.

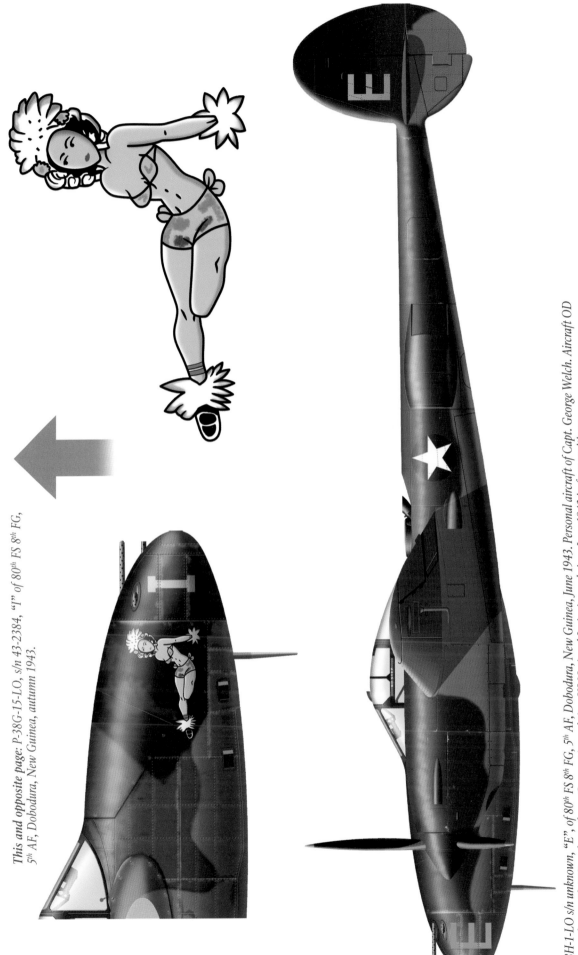

This and opposite page: P-38G-15-LO, s/n 43-2384, "I" of 80th FS 8th FG, 5th AF, Dobodura, New Guinea, autumn 1943.

P-38H-1-LO s/n unknown, "E", of 80th FS 8th FG, 5th AF, Dobodura, New Guinea, June 1943. Personal aircraft of Capt. George Welch. Aircraft OD uppersurfaces with NG undersurfaces. Green spinners' tips. US National Insignia used since June 1943 in four positions.

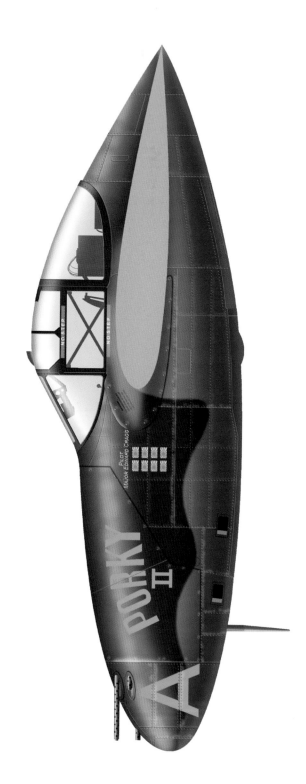

P-38H-1-LO s/n 42-66506, "A", "Porky II" of 80th FS 8th FG, 5th AF, Dobodura, New Guinea, autumn 1943. Aircraft OD uppersurfaces with NG undersurfaces. Green spinners' tips. US National Insignia used since August 1943 in four positions. Red border on the aircraft name is speculative (shown on the lower drawing).

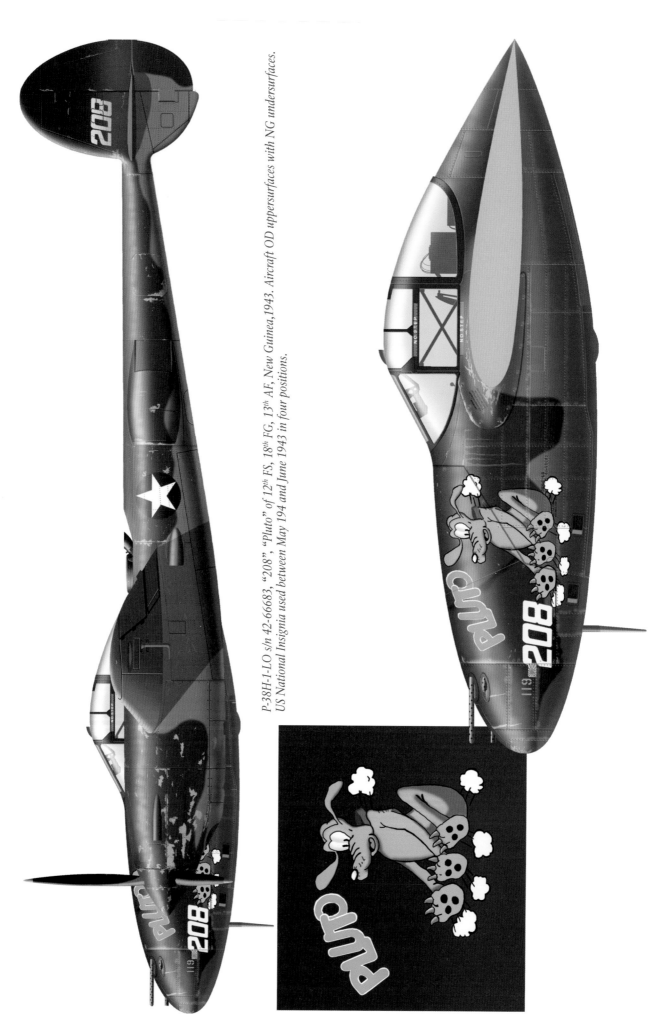

P-38H-1-LO s/n 42-66683, "208", "Pluto" of 12th FS, 18th FG, 13th AF, New Guinea, 1943. Aircraft OD uppersurfaces with NG undersurfaces. US National Insignia used between May 194 and June 1943 in four positions.

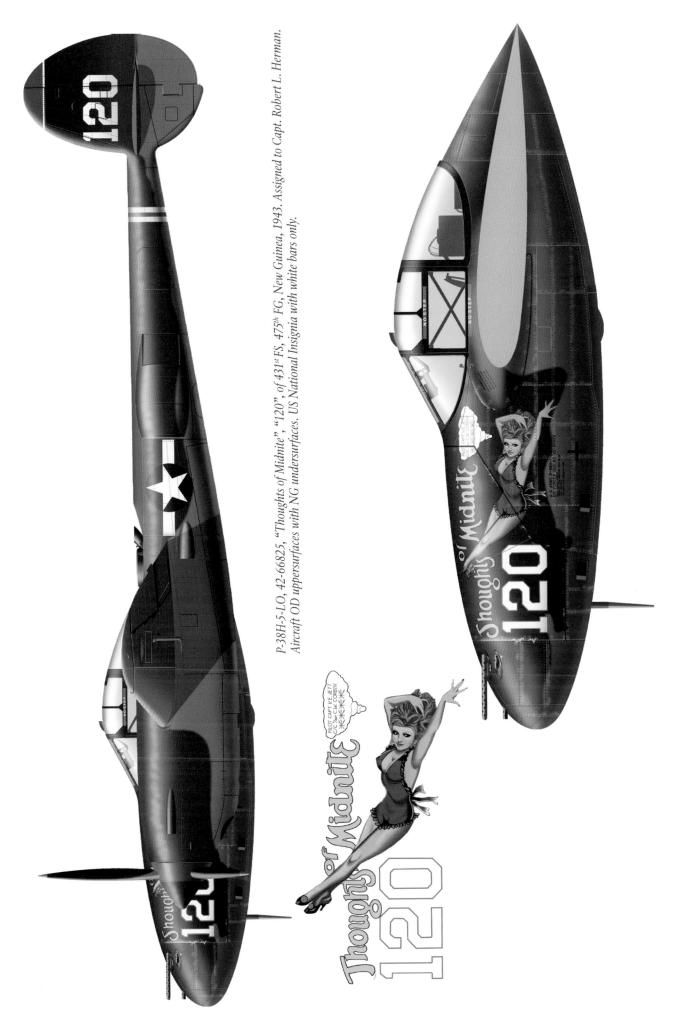

P-38H-5-LO, 42-66825, "Thoughts of Midnite", "120", of 431ˢᵗ FS, 475ᵗʰ FG, New Guinea, 1943. Assigned to Capt. Robert L. Herman. Aircraft OD uppersurfaces with NG undersurfaces. US National Insignia with white bars only.

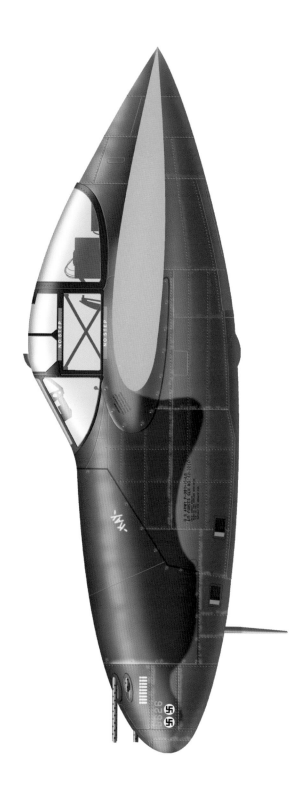

P-38G-15-LO s/n 42-32517 of 37th FS 14th FG. North Africa, June 1943. Aircraft OD uppersurfaces with NG undersurfaces. US National Insignia with yellow border (used during Operation Torch) in four positions.

P-38H-5-LO s/n 42-67060, CG-S, "Skylark IV" of 38th FS, 55th FG. Nunshapnead, England, November 1943. Assigned to Maj. Mark K. Shipman. Aircraft OD uppersurfaces with NG undersurfaces. US National Insignia with bars and red border as used between June 1943 and August 1943.

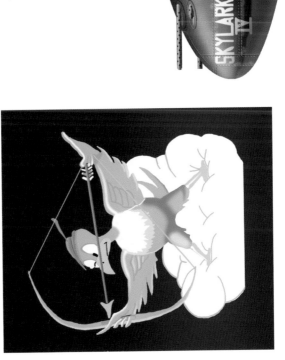

P-38H-5-LO s/n 42-66836, "131" "Pugdy" of 431ˢᵗ FS, 475ᵗʰ FG, 5ᵗʰ AF. Dobodura, October 1943. Assigned to 1ˢᵗ Lt. Thomas B. McGuire, Jr. Aircraft OD uppersurfaces with NG undersurfaces. US National Insignia with white bars only.

F-5A, "80", "Jeanne" of GR 2/33, the Free French Air Force, La Marsa Tunisia, 1943. OD uppersurafces with Sky undersurfaces. French roundels in six positions.

F-4, "40", "Stinky 2" of 9ᵗʰ Photographic Reconnaissance Squadron, 7ᵗʰ Bomb Group, Pandaveswar, India, 1943. Aircraft in Haze Paint. US National Insignia with red sorround use din 1943.

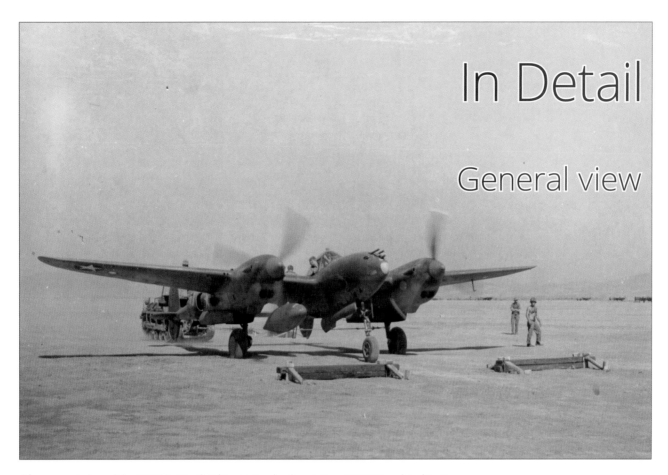

Above: Front view of the P-38G in North Africa taxing for the mission. *(US National Archives)*

Below: Lockheed P-38F-1-LO Lightning s/n 41-7630, c/n 222-5757 "Glacier Girl".
On 15 July 1942, due to poor weather, six P-38s of 94th FS, 1st FG and two B-17s were forced to return to Greenland en route to the British Isles during Operation Bolero. The aircraft were forced to make emergency landings on the ice field. All the crew members were subsequently rescued. However, "Glacier Girl", along with the unit's five other fighters and the two B-17s, were eventually buried under 268 feet (82 m) of snow and ice. In 1992, the plane was brought to the surface by members of the Greenland Expedition Society after years of searching and excavation. The aircraft was transported to Middlesboro, Kentucky, USA where it was restored to flying condition. The Lightning returned to the air in October 2002. In 2007, "Glacier Girl" was sold to Lewis Energy's CEO, Rodney Lewis. *(Steven Dickey)*

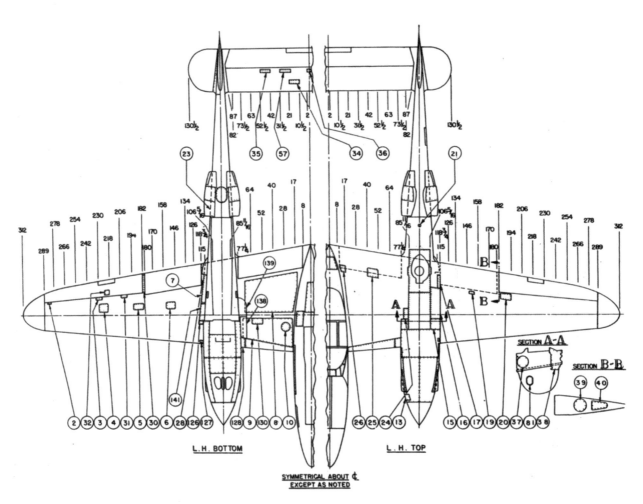

L.H. BOTTOM

L.H. TOP

SECTION A-A

SECTION B-B

SYMMETRICAL ABOUT ₵
EXCEPT AS NOTED

2	AILERON COUNTER WEIGHT	28	FLAP CABLES
3	AILERON PUSH-PULL TUBE	30	FLAP CABLES AND PULLEYS
4	AILERON DIFFERENTIAL MECHANISM	31	TAB IDLER PULLEY
5	TAB PULLEY	32	TAB ACTUATING MECHANISM LUBRICATION
6	AILERON AND TAB TURNBUCKLE	34	RUDDER TAB STOP
7	WING JOINT	35	ELEVATOR TAB STOP (L.H. ONLY)
8	FUEL TANK INSPECTION	36	ELEVATOR TAB ACTUATING MECHANISM
9	FUEL TANK INSPECTION	37	EMPENNAGE CONTROL CABLES
10	FUEL DRAIN	38	WING PINS
13	PRESTONE FILLER CAP (R.H. SIDE BOTH NACELLES)	39	FLAP CABLES
15	ENGINE OIL	40	FLAP CABLES
16	WING JOINT	57	TAB CABLE TURNBUCKLE (L.H. ONLY)
17	FLAP CABLES	81	ENGINE MOUNT BAY STRUT ATTACHMENT
19	FLAP CABLES	126	INTERCOOLER ATTACHMENT BOLT
20	TAB CABLES	127	ENGINE MOUNT BOLT
21	LIFT LUG	128	ENGINE MOUNT FITTING & PLUMBING
23	COOLANT TUBE JOINT	130	ENGINE CONTROL CABLES
24	LIFT LUG	138	FAIRING
25	FLAP CABLES	139	FAIRING
26	FLAP CABLES	141	FILLET JUNCTION BOX

REFER TO DWG. 233546

This and opposite page:
P-38H inspection panels.
(P-38 Technical Manual)

Opposite page bottom:
Starboard side of the P-38F "Glacier
Girl" (Steven Dickey)

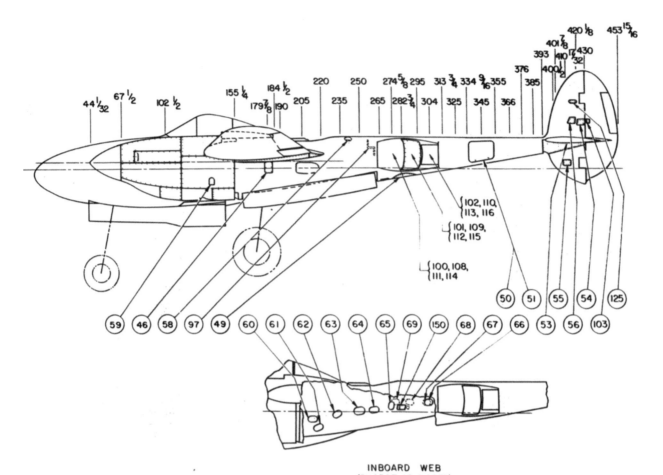

INBOARD WEB
(EXCEPT AS NOTED)

46 MAIN L.G. FULCRUM PIN (BOTH SIDES EACH BOOM)
49 RADIATOR FLAP CYLINDER
50 BAGGAGE AND TOOLS (L.H. SIDE RIGHT BOOM)
51 BATTERIES (L.H. BOOM OUTBOARD)
53 EMPENNAGE CONTROLS
54 TAB ACTUATING UNIT (L.H. SIDE EACH FIN)
55 ELEVATOR PULLEYS (L.H. SIDE EACH FIN)
56 ELEVATOR PULLEYS
58 SUPERCHARGER OIL
59 STARTER EXTENSION (R.H. SIDE BOTH NACELLES)
60 COOLANT TUBE
61 COOLANT TUBE
62 COOLANT TUBE
63 COOLANT TUBE AND EMPENNAGE SURFACE CONTROLS
64 TAB CABLE
65 COOLANT TUBE AND TAB CABLE
66 COOLANT TUBE AND TAB CABLE
67 COOLANT TUBE (OUTBOARD WEB)

68 COOLANT TUBE (OUTBOARD WEB)
69 COOLANT TUBE (OUTBOARD WEB)
97 STARTER CRANK INSIDE (L.H. OUTBOARD BOOM ONLY)
100 COOLANT SCOOP (L.H. BOOM OUTBOARD)
101 RADIATOR SHROUD (L.H. BOOM OUTBOARD)
102 RADIATOR FLAP (L.H. BOOM OUTBOARD)
103 TAB ACTUATING UNIT
108 COOLANT SCOOP (L.H. BOOM INBOARD)
109 RADIATOR SHROUD (L.H. BOOM INBOARD)
110 RADIATOR FLAP (L.H. BOOM INBOARD)
111 COOLANT SCOOP (R.H. BOOM OUTBOARD)
112 RADIATOR SHROUD (R.H. BOOM OUTBOARD)
113 RADIATOR FLAP (R.H. BOOM OUTBOARD)
114 COOLANT SCOOP (R.H. BOOM INBOARD)
115 RADIATOR SHROUD (R.H. BOOM INBOARD)
116 RADIATOR FLAP (R.H. BOOM INBOARD)
125 IDENTIFICATION LIGHT (INBOARD SIDE OF EACH FIN)
150 UPLOCK INSPECTION COVERS (INBOARD WEB)

Above: P-38G photographed in Algeria, 1943.
Below: P-38F-15, s/n 43-2136 of 27th FS, 1st FG, Italy. Note that "7163" – shorthand for the original Lockheed construction number, 222-7613 is visible. (Both US National Archives)

Above: Front view of the P-38F "Glacier Girl" (Steven Dickey)

Below: F-5A, "35" photographed over the North Africa, 1943. (US National Archives)

Above: Port side of the
P-38F "Glacier Girl"
(Steven Dickey)

Right: Gen. James
H. Doolittle in the
cockpit of P-38H-5-LO
s/n 42-66972, "some-
where in England"
after returning from the
Mediterranean to take
command of the 8th AF.
(US National Archives)

Main fuselage

Above: Port side of the P-38F "Glacier Girl" nose. (Steven Dickey)

Below: P-38 used for the technicians training in the 8th AF workshop. (US National Archives)

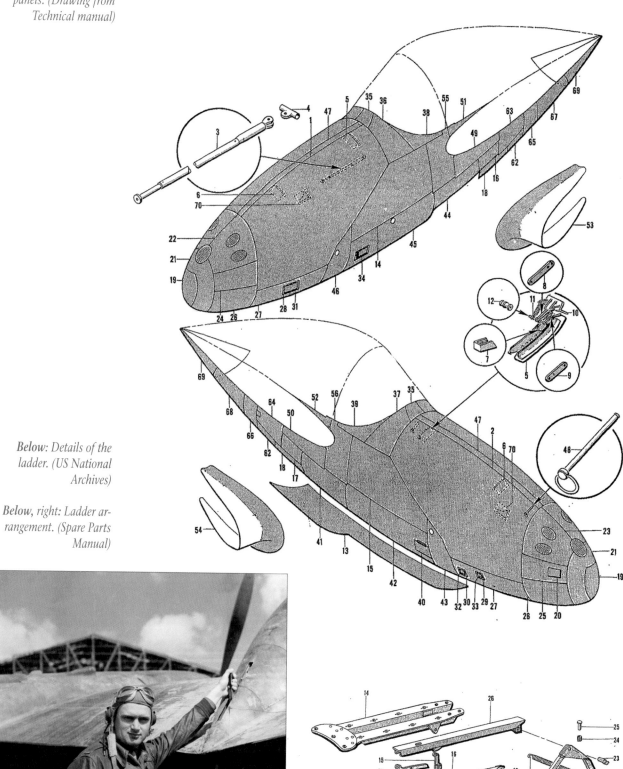

P-38 main fuselage panels. (Drawing from Technical manual)

Below: Details of the ladder. (US National Archives)

Below, right: Ladder arrangement. (Spare Parts Manual)

Above: P-38G, "88", "Elsie" crashed at Dobodura, New Guinea, 5 April 1943.

Below, left: P-38 "Jinx" Aircraft assigned to Col. Robert Richard, 1ˢᵗ FG commander 19 September 1943 to 14 November 1944. (Both US National Archives)

Below, right: Navigation light mounted under the central fuselage. (Technical Manual)

P-38 front view. Pilots of the 96th FS, 82nd FG after combat over Sicily.

Port side of the main fuselage. P-38G-15, "75", "EARTHQUAKE MC-GOON", photographed in North Africa, August 1943. Lt. Richard A. Campbell, Ferriday. 37th FS, 14th FG.

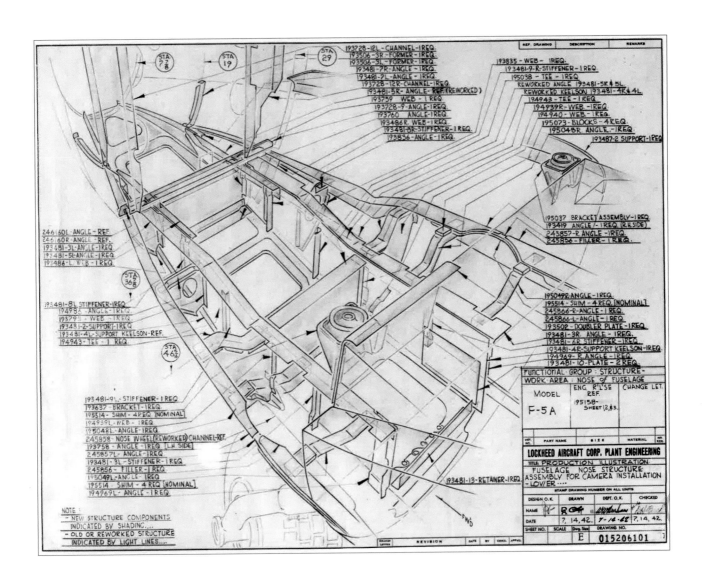

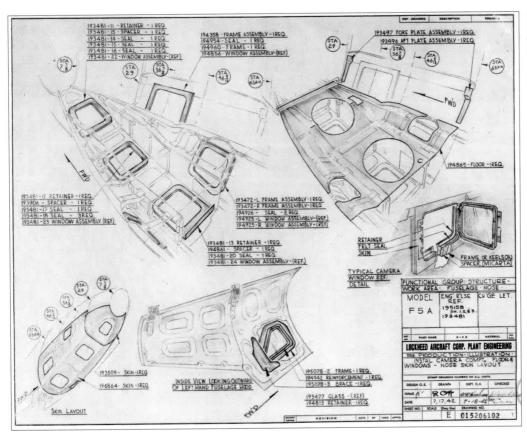

Two drawings of the F-4 main fuselage construction. (Technical Manual)

Tail booms

Above: Starboard tail boom of the P-38F.

Right: Port engine coolant radiator. Exhaust door in the open position.

Turbo-supercharger intake, port side. Note the red cover with "Remove before flight sign". (All Steven Dickey)

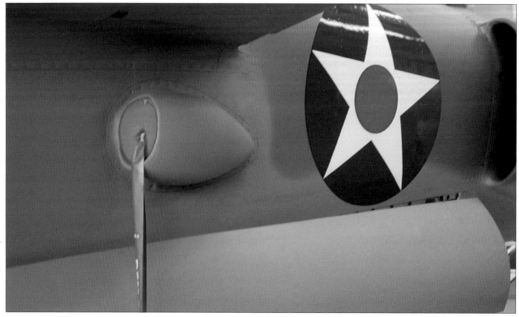

Above: General Electric Type B3 turbosupercharger is visible in the centre of the photo. Two small supercharger cooling intakes are in front of the supercharger, while the scoop at the front (silver), at the front feeds the cockpit heater.

Below: Port tail boom. Engine coolant radiator exhaust door in the fully open position.
(Both Steven Dickey)

Two photo of the engine coolant radiator details. (Technical manual)

224191 EXIT FLAP

224165 RADIATOR ASSEMBLY

AFT BOOM

224077 SCOOP ASSEMBLY

224359 SKIN ASSEMBLY

REFER TO DWG. NO. 236287

Port tail boom. Detail of the boom – tail joint is visible. (Steven Dickey)

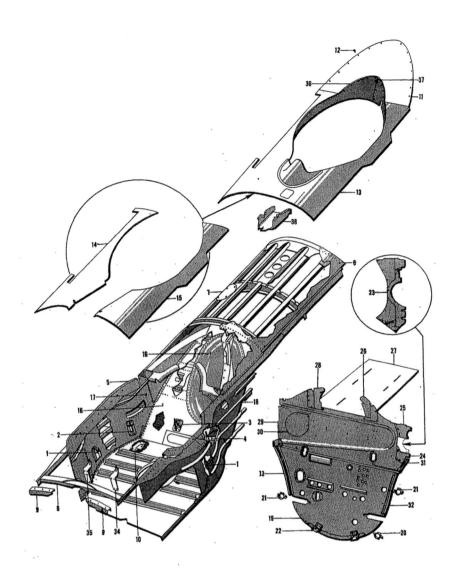

Supercharger housing and covers details.

Bottom, left: *Port tail boom construction.*

Bottom, right: *Tail booms skinning. (All drawings Technical Manual)*

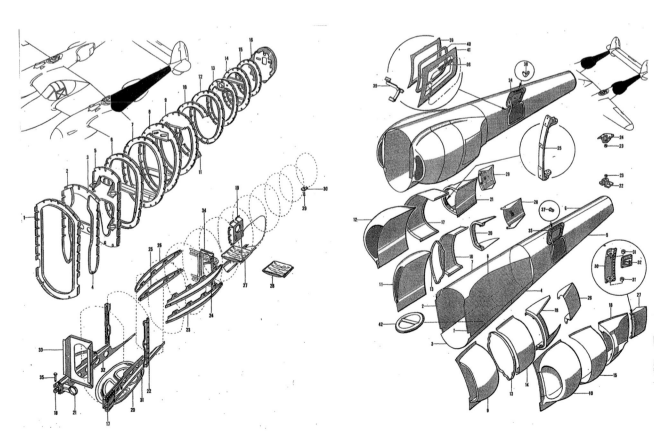

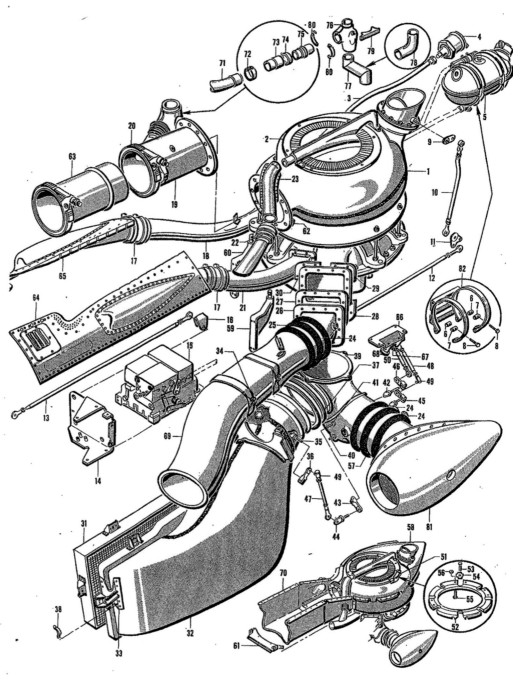

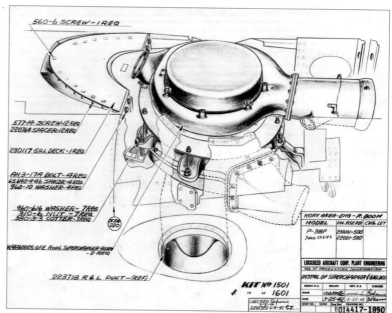

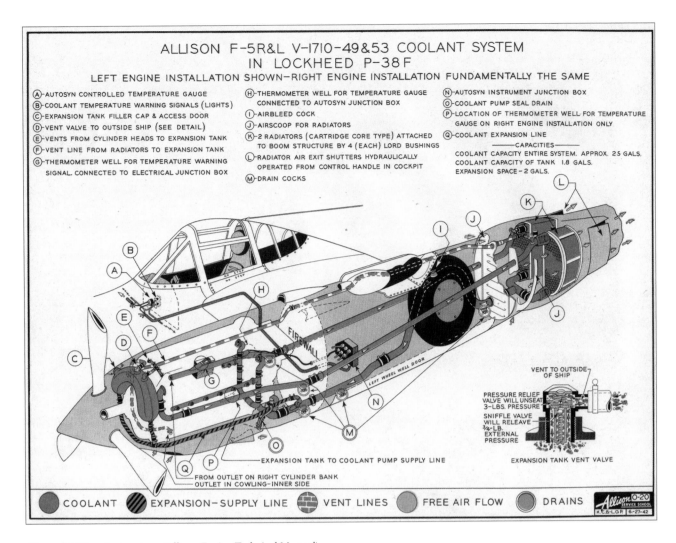

ALLISON F-5R&L V-1710-49&53 COOLANT SYSTEM IN LOCKHEED P-38F
LEFT ENGINE INSTALLATION SHOWN—RIGHT ENGINE INSTALLATION FUNDAMENTALLY THE SAME

Ⓐ-AUTOSYN CONTROLLED TEMPERATURE GAUGE
Ⓑ-COOLANT TEMPERATURE WARNING SIGNALS (LIGHTS)
Ⓒ-EXPANSION TANK FILLER CAP & ACCESS DOOR
Ⓓ-VENT VALVE TO OUTSIDE SHIP (SEE DETAIL)
Ⓔ-VENTS FROM CYLINDER HEADS TO EXPANSION TANK
Ⓕ-VENT LINE FROM RADIATORS TO EXPANSION TANK
Ⓖ-THERMOMETER WELL FOR TEMPERATURE WARNING
   SIGNAL. CONNECTED TO ELECTRICAL JUNCTION BOX

Ⓗ-THERMOMETER WELL FOR TEMPERATURE GAUGE
   CONNECTED TO AUTOSYN JUNCTION BOX
Ⓘ-AIRBLEED COCK
Ⓙ-AIRSCOOP FOR RADIATORS
Ⓚ-2 RADIATORS (CARTRIDGE CORE TYPE) ATTACHED
   TO BOOM STRUCTURE BY 4 (EACH) LORD BUSHINGS
Ⓛ-RADIATOR AIR EXIT SHUTTERS HYDRAULICALLY
   OPERATED FROM CONTROL HANDLE IN COCKPIT
Ⓜ-DRAIN COCKS

Ⓝ-AUTOSYN INSTRUMENT JUNCTION BOX
Ⓞ-COOLANT PUMP SEAL DRAIN
Ⓟ-LOCATION OF THERMOMETER WELL FOR TEMPERATURE
   GAUGE ON RIGHT ENGINE INSTALLATION ONLY
Ⓠ-COOLANT EXPANSION LINE
   ——CAPACITIES——
   COOLANT CAPACITY ENTIRE SYSTEM. APPROX. 25 GALS.
   COOLANT CAPACITY OF TANK 1.8 GALS.
   EXPANSION SPACE—2 GALS.

VENT TO OUTSIDE OF SHIP

PRESSURE RELIEF VALVE WILL UNSEAT 3-LBS. PRESSURE
SNIFFLE VALVE WILL RELEAVE ¾-LB. EXTERNAL PRESSURE

EXPANSION TANK VENT VALVE

EXPANSION TANK TO COOLANT PUMP SUPPLY LINE
FROM OUTLET ON RIGHT CYLINDER BANK
OUTLET IN COWLING—INNER SIDE

⬤ COOLANT   ▨ EXPANSION—SUPPLY LINE   ⬤ VENT LINES   ⬤ FREE AIR FLOW   ⬤ DRAINS

Allison O-20 SERVICE SCHOOL K.C.B.-L.O.P. 6-27-42

Above: P-38F coolant system. (Allison Engine Technical Manual)

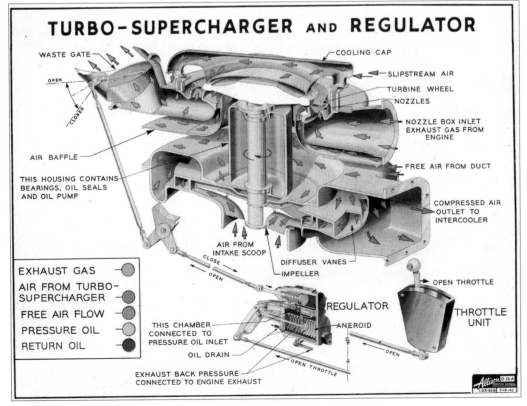

TURBO-SUPERCHARGER AND REGULATOR

WASTE GATE
OPEN
CLOSED
AIR BAFFLE
THIS HOUSING CONTAINS BEARINGS, OIL SEALS AND OIL PUMP

COOLING CAP
SLIPSTREAM AIR
TURBINE WHEEL
NOZZLES
NOZZLE BOX INLET EXHAUST GAS FROM ENGINE
FREE AIR FROM DUCT
COMPRESSED AIR OUTLET TO INTERCOOLER

AIR FROM INTAKE SCOOP
CLOSE
OPEN
DIFFUSER VANES
IMPELLER

OPEN THROTTLE

REGULATOR

THROTTLE UNIT

THIS CHAMBER CONNECTED TO PRESSURE OIL INLET
OIL DRAIN
ANEROID
OPEN
OPEN THROTTLE
EXHAUST BACK PRESSURE CONNECTED TO ENGINE EXHAUST

EXHAUST GAS	⬤
AIR FROM TURBO-SUPERCHARGER	⬤
FREE AIR FLOW	⬤
PRESSURE OIL	⬤
RETURN OIL	⬤

Allison O-26-A SERVICE SCHOOL L.O.P.-S.E.E.L. 7-16-42

Turbo-Supercharger drawing from Allison Engine Technical Manual.

War time photo of an Allison engine awaiting replacement in a P-38. (US National Archives)

Two photos of an Allison engine mounted in a P-38E.
1. Rod assembly.
2. Oil separator.
3. Spark plug coolant blast tube
4. Tube.
5. Vacuum pump.
6. Generator.
7. Hose clump.
8. Shut-off valve

(Both Technical Manual)

1. Tube.
2. Propeller governor.
3. Propeller motor governor.
4. Flap assembly
5. Oil temperature regulator.
6. Duct assembly.

P-38 during engine exchange, North Africa. (US National Archives)

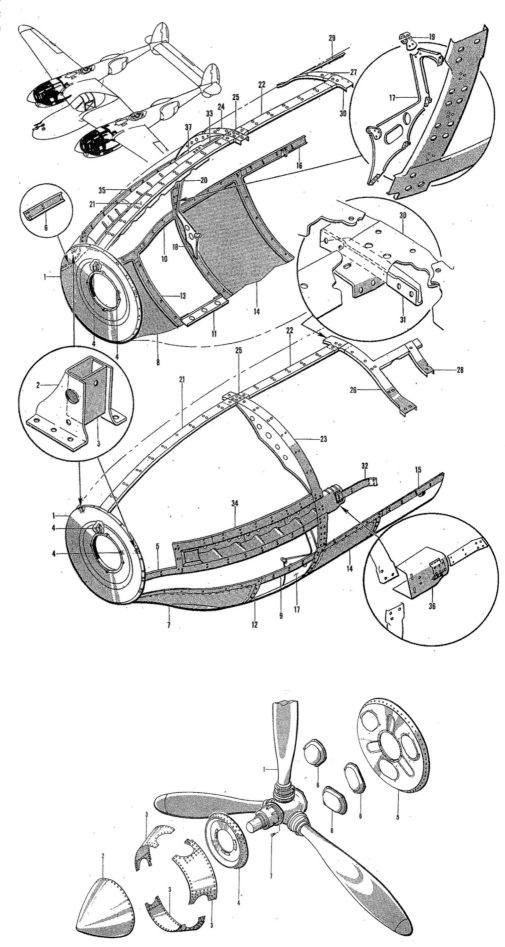

P-38H engine nacelles frames. (Spare Parts manual)

Propeller assembly. (Spare Parts Manual)

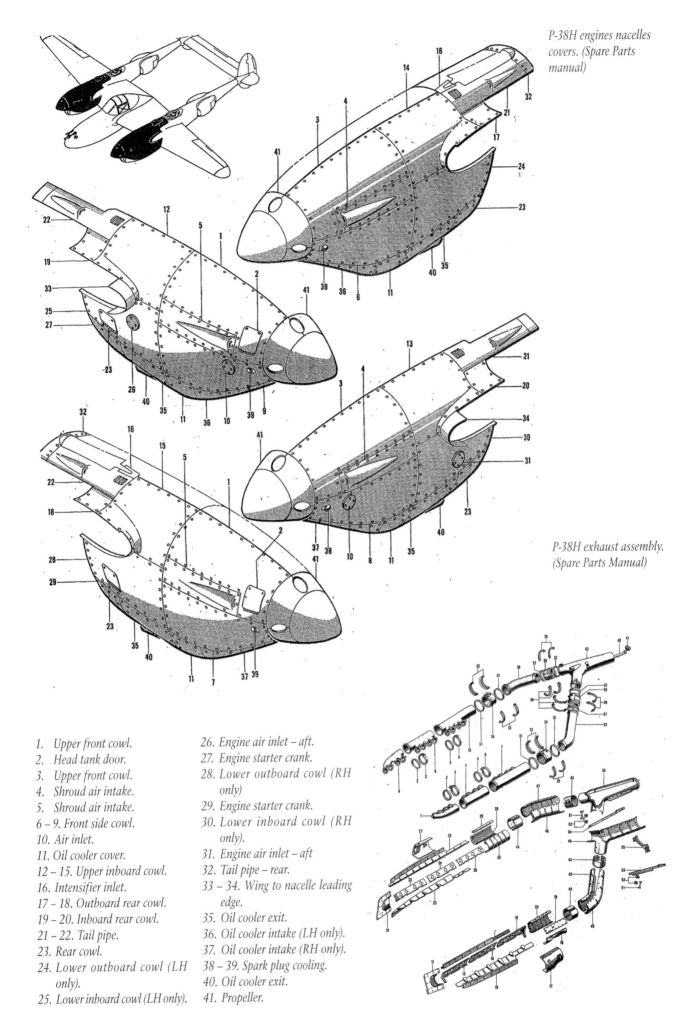

P-38H engines nacelles covers. (Spare Parts manual)

P-38H exhaust assembly. (Spare Parts Manual)

1. Upper front cowl.
2. Head tank door.
3. Upper front cowl.
4. Shroud air intake.
5. Shroud air intake.
6 – 9. Front side cowl.
10. Air inlet.
11. Oil cooler cover.
12 – 15. Upper inboard cowl.
16. Intensifier inlet.
17 – 18. Outboard rear cowl.
19 – 20. Inboard rear cowl.
21 – 22. Tail pipe.
23. Rear cowl.
24. Lower outboard cowl (LH only).
25. Lower inboard cowl (LH only).

26. Engine air inlet – aft.
27. Engine starter crank.
28. Lower outboard cowl (RH only)
29. Engine starter crank.
30. Lower inboard cowl (RH only).
31. Engine air inlet – aft
32. Tail pipe – rear.
33 – 34. Wing to nacelle leading edge.
35. Oil cooler exit.
36. Oil cooler intake (LH only).
37. Oil cooler intake (RH only).
38 – 39. Spark plug cooling.
40. Oil cooler exit.
41. Propeller.

P-38 starboard engine nacelle, inner side. 2nd Lt. Johnny Roehm 44th FS, 18th FG after returning from Rabaul on 18 January 1944, Guadalcanal.

P-38G-13-LO s/n 43-2242, "129, "Oriole" of 39th FS, 347th FG, Guadalcanal. 1st Lt. Murray J. Shubin, officially credited with eleven confirmed aerial victories. (Both US National Archives)

Canopy

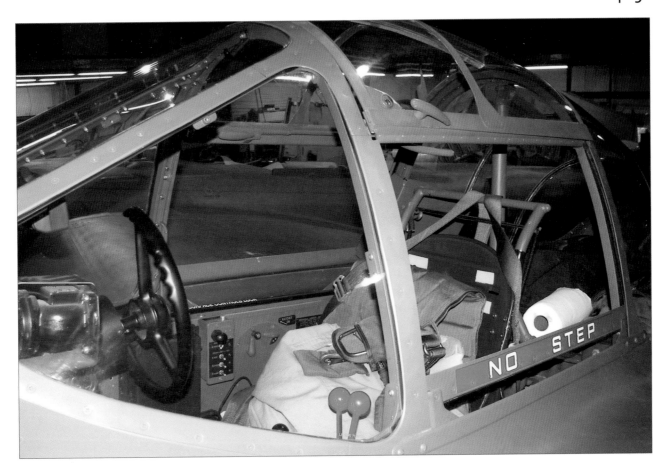

P-38F canopy, port side. Side window in closed position. (Steven Dickey)

Another photo of the P-38F canopy, port side. (Author's coll.)

Cockpit

Two modern photos of the preserved P-38F instrument panel. (Both Steven Dickey)

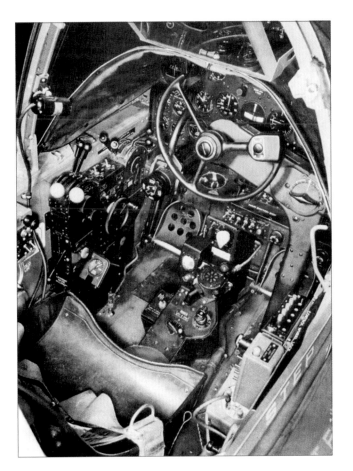

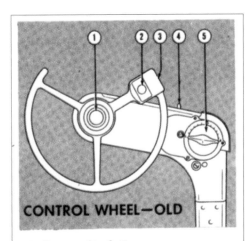

Above: P-38D instrument panel.

Below, left: P-38 E instrument panel.
(Both Lockheed)

Below, right: Drawing of the control wheel, as used in all early P-38s up to the P-38H version.

(P-38 Pilot's Manual)

CONTROL WHEEL—OLD

1. **Radio transmitter button.**
2. **Cannon trigger button.**
3. **Machine gun trigger button (back of wheel).**
4. **Gun-camera selector switch.**
5. **Aileron trim tab control.** P-38's with aileron boost do not have an aileron trim tab control.

P-38F cockpit.
(Drawing by Zbigniew Kolacha)

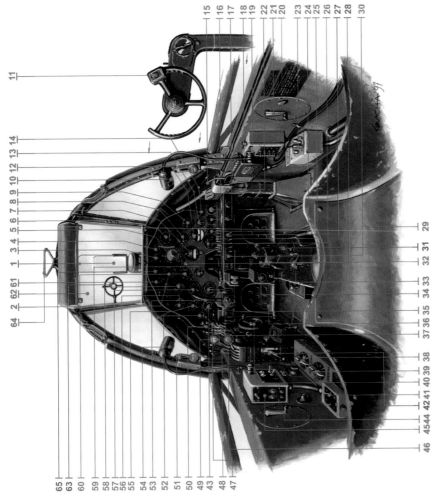

1. Reflector gunsight;
2. Airspeed indicator;
3. Ammeter;
4. Ammeter;
5. Artificial horizon;
6. Magnetic compass;
7. Directional gyro;
8. Rate of climb indicator;
9. Gyrocompass indicator;
10. Instrument panel light;
11. Microphone switch;
12. Turn and bank indicator;
13. Temperature gauge;
14. Hydraulic installation pressure gauge;
15. Flap control lever;
16. Ignition cut off;
17. Pressure gauge;
18. Radio off push button and frequency selector push buttons;
19. Cockpit light and recognition light switches;
20. Window crank hatched handles;
21. Starboard window crank;
22. Control column;
23. Receiver control box;
24. Pressure gauge;
25. Switches;
26. Landing gear and flap position indicator;
27. Generator, battery switches;
28. Radio call number;
29. Pilot's seat;
30. Automatic coil cooler flap switches;
31. Engine primer;
32. Oxygen apparatus;
33. Rudder trim tab control;
34. Oxygen flow indicator;
35. Propeller feathering switches;
36. Rudder pedals;

37. Starboard engine gauge (oil temperature, oil pressure and fuel pressure);
38. Port tank selector valve;
39. Starboard tank selector valve;
40. Elevator tab control;
41. Auxiliary fuel pump switches;
42. Landing gear control handle;
43. Port engine gauge (oil temperature, oil pressure and fuel pressure);
44. Port window crank;
45. Bomb or tank release selector switches;
46. Starboard engine throttle lever;
47. Mixture controls;
48. Propeller controls;
49. Port engine throttle lever;
50. Coolant shutter controls;
51. Cockpit heating controls;
52. Main fuel tank quantity gauge;
53. External tanks emergency drop lever;
54. Instrument panel light;
55. Port engine tachometer;
56. Dual manifold pressure gauge (starboard engine);
57. Starboard engine tachometer;
58. Dual manifold pressure gauge (port engine);
59. Mixture temperature gauge
60. Altimeter;
61. Starboard engine coolant temperature gauge;
62. Armoured glass;
63. Gunsight for Bazooka rocket launchers;
64. Hatch release handle;
65. Port engine coolant temperature gauge.

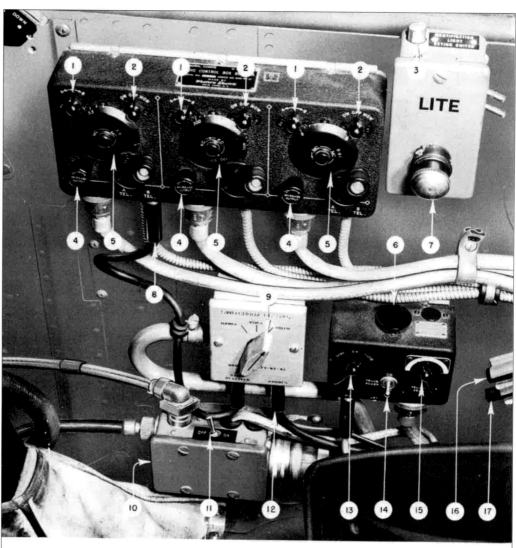

P-38F radio controls.
(Technical Manual)

1. HEADSET SELECTOR SWITCH
2. RECEIVER CONTROL SWITCH
3. IDENTIFICATION LIGHT KEYING SWITCH
4. RECEIVER VOLUME CONTROLS
5. RECEIVER TUNING DIAL AND CRANK
6. TRANSMITTER KEY
7. COCKPIT LIGHT
8. TELEPHONE PLUG—PLUGGED IN "B" JACK
9. RADIO RANGE SELECTOR SWITCH

10. RADIO JUNCTION BOX
11. CONTACTOR HEATER SWITCH
12. HEADSET JACK—EXTENSION CORD PLUGGED IN
13. TRANSMITTER CONTROL SWITCH
14. TRANSMITTER POWER SWITCH
15. TRANSMITTER SELECTOR SWITCH
16. MICROPHONE JACK—STOWED
17. HEADSET—EXTENSION CORD JACK STOWED

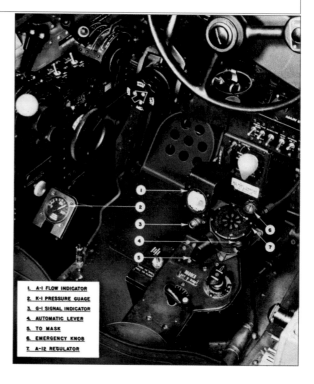

1. A-1 FLOW INDICATOR
2. K-1 PRESSURE GUAGE
3. G-1 SIGNAL INDICATOR
4. AUTOMATIC LEVER
5. TO MASK
6. EMERGENCY KNOB
7. A-12 REGULATOR

P-38F oxygen installation controls.
(Technical Manual)

Rear cockpit radio installation.
1. *BC-454A receiver,*
2. *BS-453A receiver.*
3. *BC-455A receiver.*
4. *BC-442A antenna relay unit.*
5. *457A transmitter.*
6. *DM-33A dynamotor.*
7. *BC-456A modular unit.*
8. *459A transmitter.*

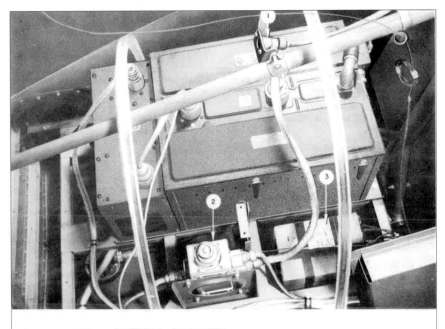

Two photos of SCR-522A radio installation. (All Technical Manual)

1. UPWARD RECOGNITION LIGHT
2. JB-29A JUNCTION BOX
3. RANGE RECEIVER BATTERY
4. SCR-522-A RADIO CONTROLS
5. RECOGNITION LIGHTS KEYING SWITCH
6. COCKPIT LIGHT
7. RECOGNITION LIGHTS SELECTOR SWITCHE
8. RCA-AVR-101 BEACON RECEIVER

B. COCKPIT CONTROLS

Above: Starboard side of the preserved P-38F cockpit. Note that original radio control is replaced by the modern one (black box).

Below: Port side of the preserved P-38F cockpit. Engine control panel is visible.
(Both Steven Dickey)

*Above: P-38F instru-
ment panel. (Pilot's
Manual)*

*Instrument panel as
used in the "British"
version of the P-38.
(Pilot's Manual)*

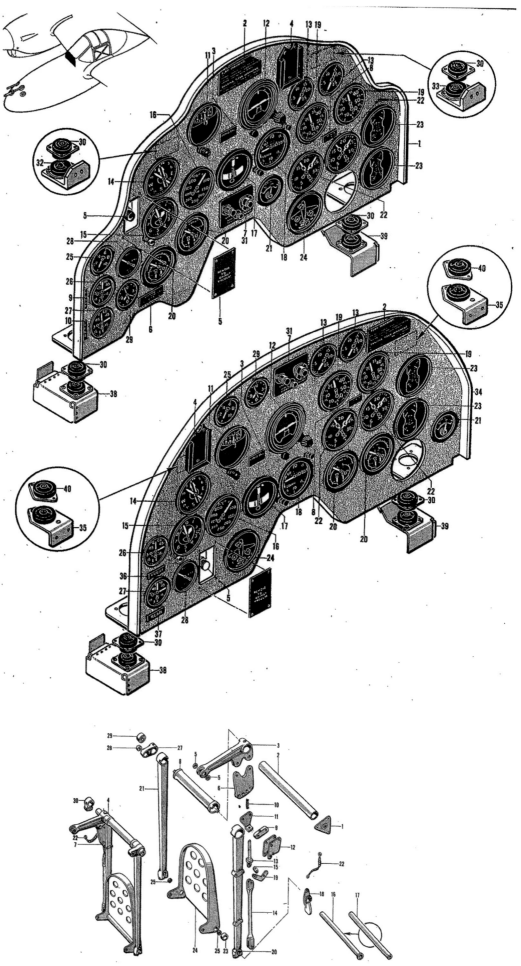

Two versions of the instrument panels used on the P-38H. Early production version (above). Late production version (below). (Spare Parts Manual)

Rudder pedals assembly of P-38H. (Spare Parts Manual)

F-4 cockpit.
1. Blinker light panel.
2. Camera compartment temperature gauge.
3. Amber light.
4. Photographic equipment master switch.
5. Chart intervalometer switch.
6. Reconnaissance intervalometer switch.
7. Blinker light switch.
8. Camera control button (aft of the wheel shown).
9. Vaccum control lever.
10. Intervalometer (chart shown).
(Pilot's manual)

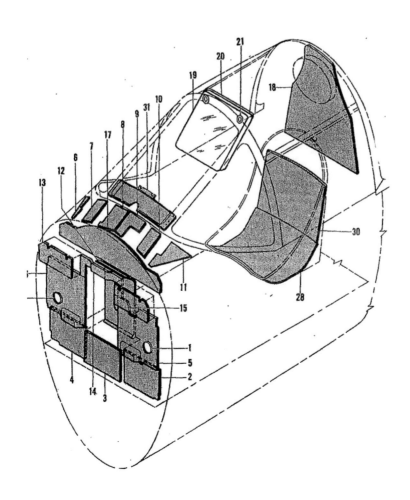

P-38H pilot's armour.
(Technical Manual)

105

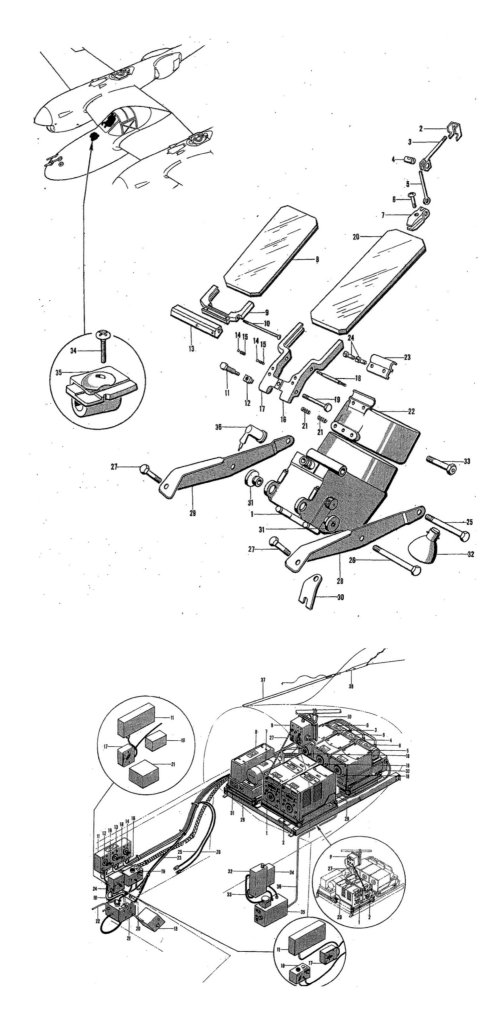

Gun sight as mounted in P-38H. (Spare Part Manual)

P-38H radio gear. (Spare Parts manual)

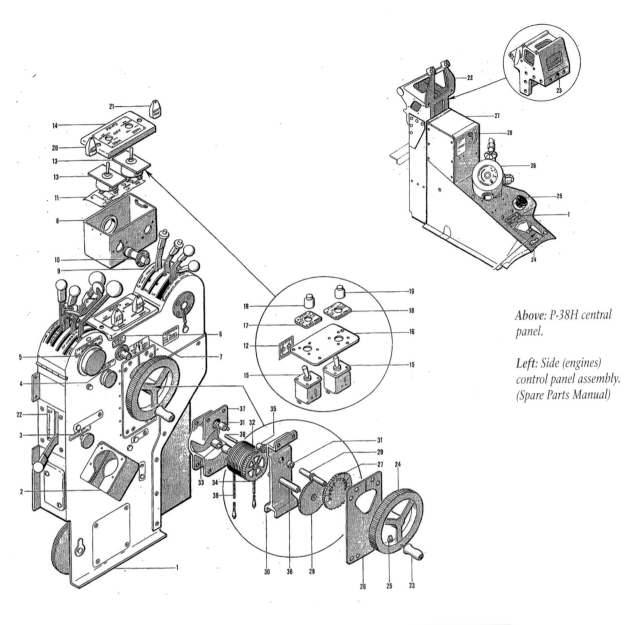

Above: P-38H central panel.

Left: Side (engines) control panel assembly. (Spare Parts Manual)

Side (engines) control panel in the preserved P-38F. (Steven Dickey)

Wing

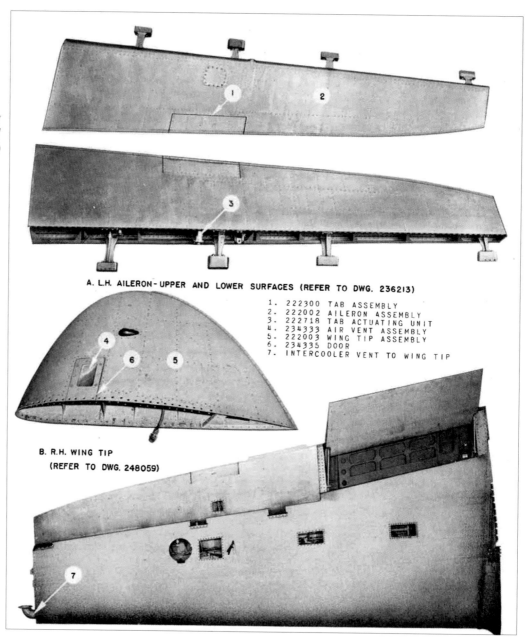

Photo of the P-38 wing assembly. (Technical Manual)

A. L.H. AILERON - UPPER AND LOWER SURFACES (REFER TO DWG. 236213)

1. 222300 TAB ASSEMBLY
2. 222002 AILERON ASSEMBLY
3. 222718 TAB ACTUATING UNIT
4. 234333 AIR VENT ASSEMBLY
5. 222003 WING TIP ASSEMBLY
6. 234335 DOOR
7. INTERCOOLER VENT TO WING TIP

B. R.H. WING TIP
(REFER TO DWG. 248059)

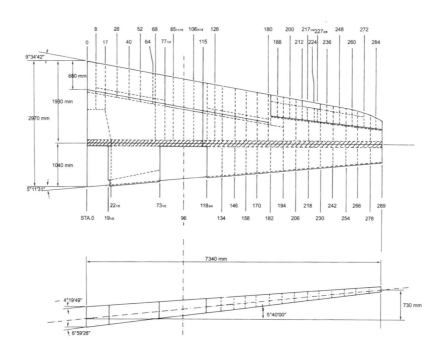

Wing stations.
(Technical Manual)

Starboard wing upper-surfaces of the P-38F. (Steven Dickey)

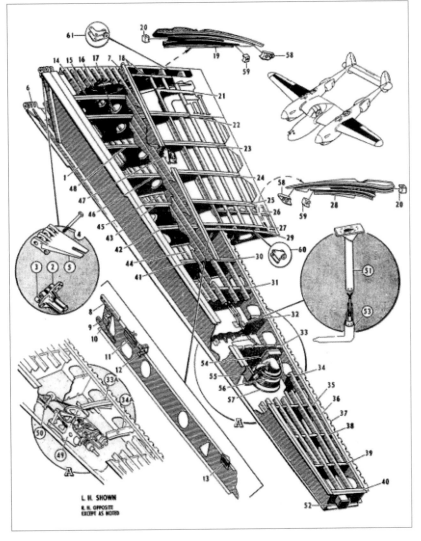

L. H. SHOWN
R. H. OPPOSITE
EXCEPT AS NOTED

Outer wing construction as shown in the P-38H Spare Parts Manual.

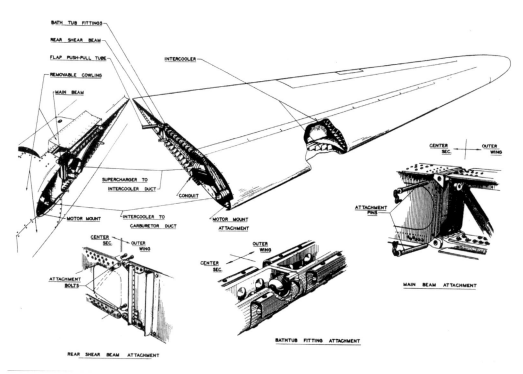

Outer wing details. (Technical Manual)

BATH TUB FITTINGS
REAR SHEAR BEAM
FLAP PUSH-PULL TUBE
REMOVABLE COWLING
MAIN BEAM
INTERCOOLER
SUPERCHARGER TO INTERCOOLER DUCT
CONDUIT
MOTOR MOUNT
INTERCOOLER TO CARBURETOR DUCT
MOTOR MOUNT ATTACHMENT
CENTER SEC.
OUTER WING
ATTACHMENT PINS
ATTACHMENT BOLTS
MAIN BEAM ATTACHMENT
REAR SHEAR BEAM ATTACHMENT
BATHTUB FITTING ATTACHMENT

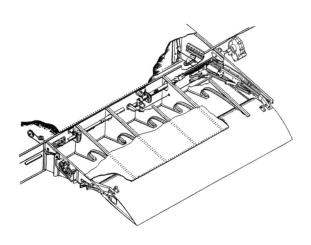

Above: Landing flap in open position. (Lockheed)

Above, right: Flap construction drawing. (Technical Manual)

Wing-central fuselage fillet introduced on P-38D, which solved the buffeting problem. (Lockheed)

Two photos of the starboard outer wing. Wing tip and navigation light is visible. (Author's coll.)

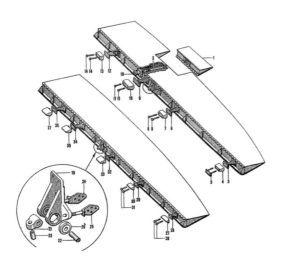

Aileron construction drawing. (Spare Parts Manual)

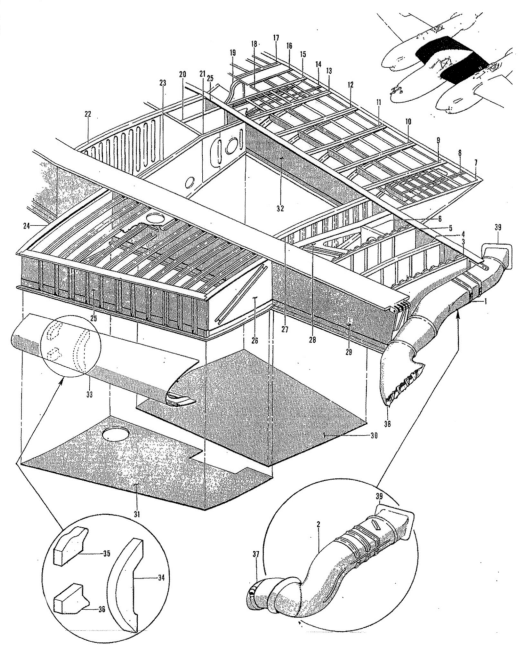

Drawing of the central wing construction. (Spare Parts Manual)

Central wing undersurfaces. (Author's coll.)

P-38E in flight showing wing uppersurfaces. (T. J. Kopański coll.)

*F-5 in flight over
North Africa.
(US National Archives)*

113

Tail

Above: Port, vertical stabiliser details of the preserved P-38F.

Right: P-38F from the rear.

(Both Steven Dickey)

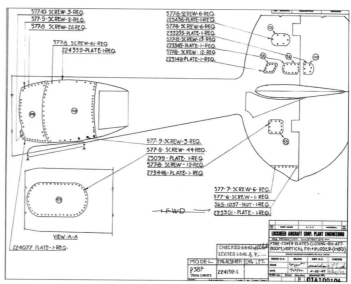

Lockheed factory drawing showing tail and tail boom removable panels.

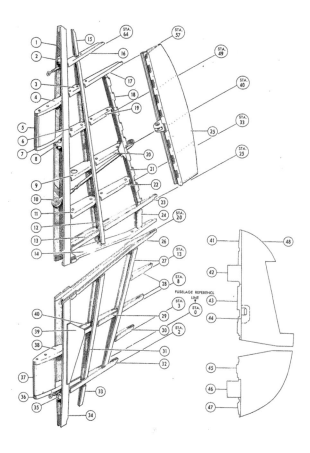

Close up shot of the vertical stabiliser and rudder. Panels are removed. Note tail skid. (Technical manual)

Above: *Rudder construction. (Spare Part Manual)*

Below: *Lower part of the stabiliser and rudder. Note modern registration in black (NX17630). (Steven Dickey)*

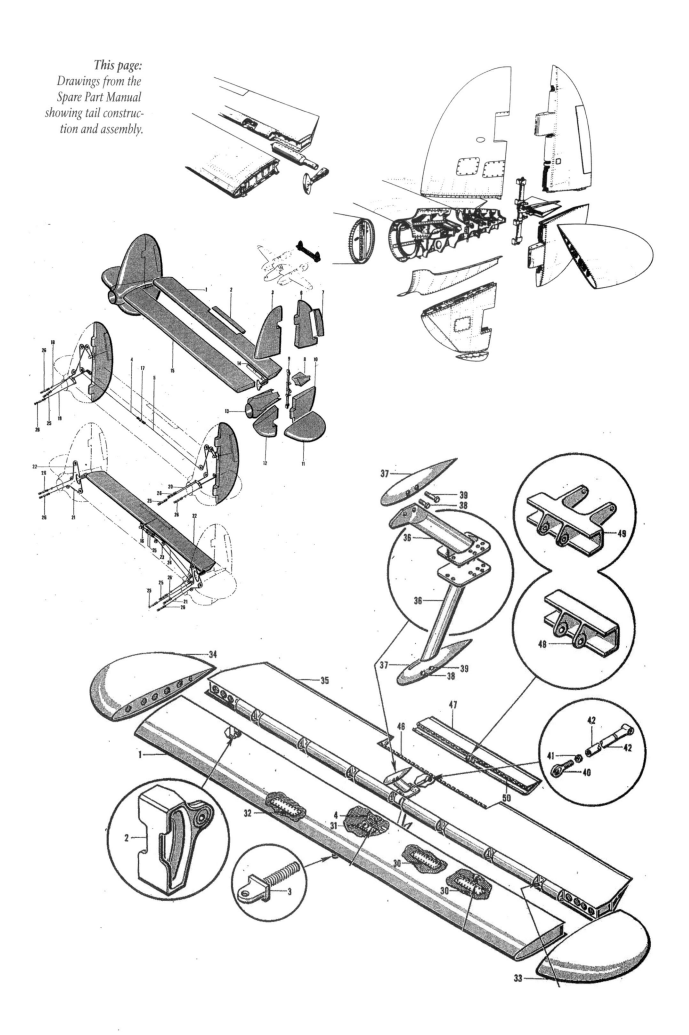

Above: Two photos of the preserved P-38F port stabiliser and rudder. (Both Steven Dickey)

Below: Inner side of the starboard stabiliser and rudder, note that port and starboard version were identical. (US National Archives)

Undercarriage

P-38F undercarriage arrangement. (Steven Dickey)

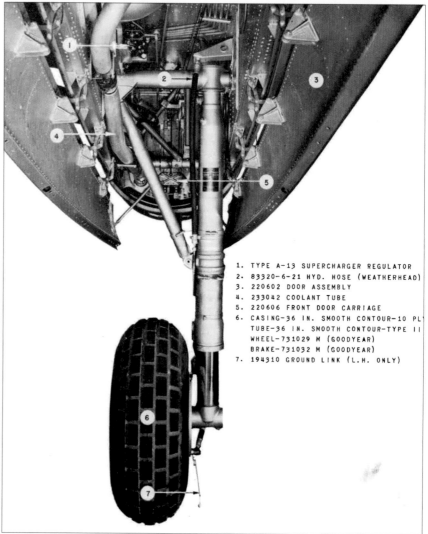

1. TYPE A-13 SUPERCHARGER REGULATOR
2. 83320-6-21 HYD. HOSE (WEATHERHEAD)
3. 220602 DOOR ASSEMBLY
4. 233042 COOLANT TUBE
5. 220606 FRONT DOOR CARRIAGE
6. CASING-36 IN. SMOOTH CONTOUR-10 PLY
   TUBE-36 IN. SMOOTH CONTOUR-TYPE II
   WHEEL-731029 M (GOODYEAR)
   BRAKE-731032 M (GOODYEAR)
7. 194310 GROUND LINK (L.H. ONLY)

Photo from the Technical manual showing the main undercarriage details.

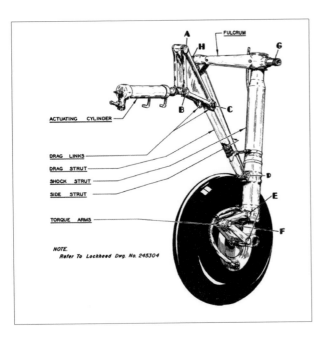

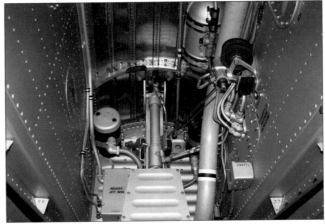

Above: Main wheel well of the preserved P-38F.
Left: Main undercarriage construction

Above: The plate is bolted over the main actuator on "Glacier Girl". This plate was fitted only to some P-38s. See photo to the left, where plate is missing. (Steven Dickey)

Left: Photo of the P-38 main landing gear bay. (Technical Manual)

	AC SPEC. 32270 ROTARY INVERTER	8	224017 SUPERCHARGER OIL TANK
	234660 INVERTER JUNCTION BOX	9	230550-515 TUBE
	1660 OXYGEN COUPLER (SCHRADER)	10	10474 L. G. DOOR STOP VALVE (BENDIX)
	ANVDD-D VALVE (PARKER)	11	401134 UPLOCK VALVE (BENDIX)
	10455 CYLINDER (BENDIX)	12	234618 UPLOCK JUNCTION BOX
	231511 CARRIAGE	13	228315 COOLANT TUBE
	AN771-2 COCK	14	11A16 VALVE DRAIN (WEATHERHEAD)

Nose undercarriage leg details. (Steven Dickey)

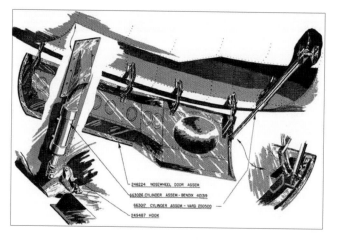

Drawing showing nose undercarriage bay door and actuator. (Technical Manual)

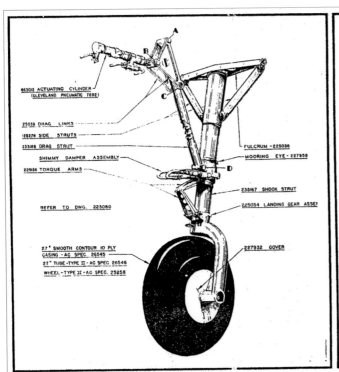

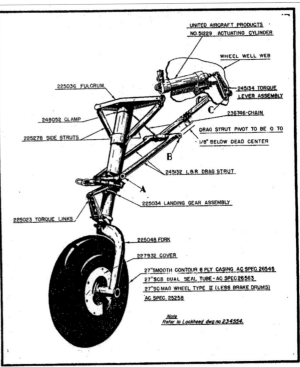

225036 FULCRUM
248052 CLAMP
225278 SIDE STRUTS
225023 TORQUE LINKS
225034 LANDING GEAR ASSEMBLY
225048 FORK
227932 COVER
27"SMOOTH CONTOUR 6 PLY CASING AC SPEC 26545
27"SCB DUAL SEAL TUBE - AC SPEC 26563
27"SQ MAG WHEEL TYPE II (LESS BRAKE DRUMS) AC SPEC 25258

UNITED AIRCRAFT PRODUCTS NO 51229 ACTUATING CYLINDER FG.
WHEEL WELL WEB
245134 TORQUE LEVER ASSEMBLY
236746-CHAIN
DRAG STRUT PIVOT TO BE O TO 1/8" BELOW DEAD CENTER
245132 L.&R DRAG STRUT

Note
Refer to Lockheed dwg no.234554.

Two drawings showing two variants of the P-38 nose undercarriage. Early – left and later introduced on P-38E, (right). (Technical Manual)

Wartime photo of the P-38 nose undercarriage. Capt. Bruno J. Virgili photographed with his Lightning of 1ˢᵗ FG. (US National Archives)

121

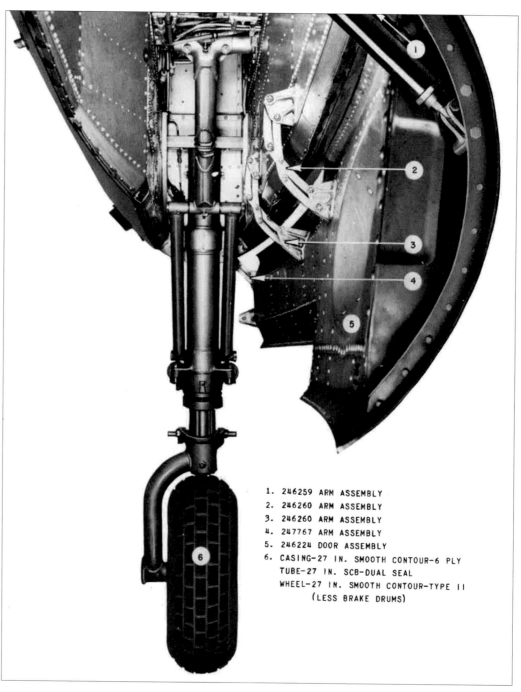

Front undercarriage gear details. (Technical Manual

1. 246259 ARM ASSEMBLY
2. 246260 ARM ASSEMBLY
3. 246260 ARM ASSEMBLY
4. 247767 ARM ASSEMBLY
5. 246224 DOOR ASSEMBLY
6. CASING-27 IN. SMOOTH CONTOUR-6 PLY
   TUBE-27 IN. SCB-DUAL SEAL
   WHEEL-27 IN. SMOOTH CONTOUR-TYPE II
   (LESS BRAKE DRUMS)

Close-up photo of nose undercarriage door and actuator. (US National Archives)

Above: Reloading of the P-38G-15-LO s/n serial 43-2482, "Babe" of 48th FS, 14th FG. (US National Archives)

Right: P-38E - armament arrangement in the nose. All later Lightnings have the same armament.
Below: P-38D armament configuration.
(Both Lockheed)

P-38F, .50 caliber ammunition canisters.

20 mm cannon ammunition canister.

Details of the 20 mm cannon.
(All photos Steven Dickey)

Close-up shot of the 20 mm cannon ammunition canister.

P-38F blast tubes details.
(Both Steven Dickey)

Reloading .50 caliber machine guns.
(US National Archives)

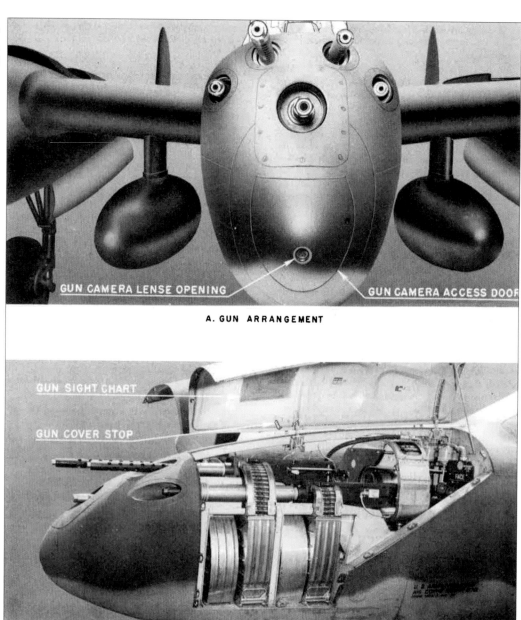

Two photos of P-38E armament arrangement. (Technical Manual)

GUN CAMERA LENSE OPENING — GUN CAMERA ACCESS DOOR

A. GUN ARRANGEMENT

GUN SIGHT CHART

GUN COVER STOP

Armament compartment shown on P-38G. Personal aircraft of 2ⁿᵈ Lt Lawrence P. Liebers, Burbank, 96ᵗʰ FS, 82ⁿᵈ FG. He was officially credited with seven confirmed aerial victories. (US National Archives)

Armament compartment shown on P-38E. (Technical Manual)

BLAST TUBE EXTENTIONS

CHATELLERAULT FEED

FEED CHUTE ADJUSTING LUG

A. GUN COVERS UP

QUICK DISCONNECT MACH.
GUN CHARGING CABLE

GUN CHARGER

CANNON AMMO. TRAY

GUN LEVELING LUGS

Armament reloading on P-38H-5-LO s/n 42-67015, CG-D of 37th FS, 14th FG. Personal aircraft of Lt Richard A. Campbell, Ferriday. (US National Archives)

Bibliography

Bell D., *Air Force Colors vol. 1*, ISBN: 0-89747-316-7, Squadron/Signal Publications Inc., 1995

Bodie W. M., *The Lockheed P-38 Lightning*, ISBN: 0-962935-90-5, Motorbooks Intl, 1991

Christy J, Ethell J., *P-38 Lightning at War*, ISBN:, Scribner, 1978

Davis L., *P-38 Lightning in action number 109*, ISBN: 0-89747-255-1, Squadron/Signal Publications Inc., 1990

Davis L., *Walk Around P-38 Lightning*, ISBN: 0-89747-453-8, Squadron/Signal Publications Inc., 2003

Freeman R., *American Eagles P-38 Lightning*, ISBN: 1-903223-17-2, Classic Publications, 2001

Jarski A., Janowicz K., *Lockheed P-38 Lightning Cz. 1*, ISBN: 83-7237-082-6, AJ-Press, 2001

Jarski A., Kolacha Z., *Lockheed P-38 Lightning Cz. 3*, ISBN: 83-7237-099-0, AJ-Press, 2002

Johnsen F. A., *Lockheed P-38 Lightning - Warbird Tech Vol. 2*, ISBN: 978-0933424-65-4, Specialty Press, 1996

Kinzey B., *P-38 Lightning in detail & scale, Part 1.*, ISBN: 1-888974-10-9, Squadron/Signal Publications Inc., 1998

Luranc Z., *Skrzydła w miniaturze nr 4-6*, ISBN: 37766X, Avia-Press, 1992

Scutts J., *Lockheed P-38 Ligthning*, ISBN: 1-86126-770-3, Crowood, 2006

Stafford G. B., *P-38 Lightning in action number 25*, ISBN: 0-89747-024-9, Squadron/Signal Publications Inc., 1976

Stanaway J., *P-38 Lightning Aces 1942-43*, ISBN: 978-1782003328, Osprey Publishing, 2014

Stanaway J., *P-38 Lightning Aces of the ETO/MTO*, ISBN: 978-1855326989, Osprey Publishing, 1998

Stanaway J., *P-38 Lightning Aces of the Pacific and CBI*, ISBN: 978-1855326330, Osprey Publishing, 1997

Fighter Gunnery, Army Air Forces Training Command, 1943

Hanbook of Service Instructions for the Lightning I Aeroplane, The Commanding General, Army Air Forces, 1942

P-38D, E, F, F-1 and F-4 Airplanes. Service Instructions, The Commanding General, Army Air Forces, 1942

Part Catalog for Airplane Model P-38H, P-38J, P-38L and F-5B, US War and Navy Departments, 1944

Pilot Training Manual for the P-38, Army Air Forces, 1944

Pilot's Flight Operating Instructions for P-38D through P-38G series, The Commanding General, Army Air Forces, 1942

Pilot's Flight Operating Instructions for P-38H..., The Commanding General, Army Air Forces, 1943

Structural Repair Instructions. P-38 Series, The Commanding General, Army Air Forces, 1943